Complete 12-week Spoken English Course

How to Use this Course

Course Outline:

- Before the course begins perform an initial assessment with each student to check that they are at a suitable level for the course, and then enrol them onto the course. This course is aimed at students who are at a good elementary level or pre-intermediate level. For this course we recommend that there are no more than ten students per class.

- The course is divided into twelve three-hour lessons. The first ten lessons each have a different topic; while lesson 11 is intended for the revision of material studied over the ten weeks, and lesson 12 is reserved for the students' examinations and an end of course review. We recommend that you hold one lesson per week, making this a twelve week course comprising 30 guided learning hours, plus 6 hours of guided revision and examination. It's up to you what order you do the lessons in; you don't have to follow our order of topics!

- If your students need more than three hours of study per week, why not offer them two 3-hour lessons per week: one Talk a Lot lesson, as described below, and one lesson using traditional teaching methods, which include conventional reading, writing and grammar-based activities that could complement the intensive speaking and listening work of the Talk a Lot lessons. You could follow a standard EFL or ESL course book such as New English File or New Headway, using material that complements the Talk a Lot lesson, so that in Week 2, for example, both 3-hour lessons are on the subject of Food and Drink. This would then give you a course with 60 guided learning hours.

- The lesson topics are:

    | Lesson 1 | Town |
    | Lesson 2 | Food |
    | Lesson 3 | Shopping |
    | Lesson 4 | Health |
    | Lesson 5 | Transport |
    | Lesson 6 | Clothes |
    | Lesson 7 | Work |
    | Lesson 8 | Family |
    | Lesson 9 | Home |
    | Lesson 10 | Free Time |
    | Lesson 11 | Revision |
    | Lesson 12 | Exam & End of Course Review |

Lesson Outline

- In our lesson outline, each lesson lasts for three hours (180 teaching minutes). This can vary according to your needs, for example, in some English language classrooms one teaching hour is equal to 45 minutes, and so 3 teaching hours would be 2¼ hours. Or it may be that you have only 2 hours per week with your group of students. You can still use Talk a Lot activities to serve up a satisfying and stimulating lesson – just in a shorter timeframe.

Complete 12-week Spoken English Course

How to Use this Course

- Each lesson focuses on a specific vocabulary topic, for example "Town". For each lesson the teacher can draw from seven different activities:

    Sentence Blocks
    Discussion Questions
    Role Plays
    Discussion Words
    Vocabulary Test
    Lesson Test
    Show & Tell

    It is not necessary to use every activity in every lesson. We believe that there is more material in this book for each lesson than is needed to fill 3 hours, so the teacher can mix and match, using different activities in different lessons. Similarly, it is not necessary to do the activities in the same order (as given below) in every lesson, but mix things up each time so that students don't become used to a set lesson order.

- Bearing that in mind, here is an example of how you could structure a 3-hour long Talk a Lot lesson:

15 mins	Welcome and **vocabulary test** (see page 5) based on the previous lesson's topic. The teacher reads out the twenty words to the students in their native language and they write them in English. The teacher gives back lesson tests, discusses the answers with the students, and can also ask random questions from the previous lesson's sentence blocks to check how much the students have remembered.
15 mins	The teacher introduces the topic of this lesson, for example, "Home". Each student has to **show and tell** an item to do with this topic, e.g. for "Home" a student could bring a utility bill, or a cushion from their favourite chair, and then tell the class about it. The teacher also brings something to "show and tell", and then introduces the eight new **sentence block** starting sentences and wh- questions on the board or on the handout (see page 8). It is essential that the teacher checks that the students understand the sentences, so that they are meaningful to students when they practise them later on. The teacher asks different students to model one or two of the sentence blocks, which will act as a reminder to students of how to make the sentence blocks.
20 mins	Students make the sentence blocks in pairs, for example, sitting back to back without eye contact. They don't write anything down and must not copy the sentence block starting sentences from the board. For this activity all the talk flows from the students making the sentence blocks from the starting sentences and wh- questions on the board or on the handout.
10 mins	Next, the teacher introduces the eight **discussion questions** for this lesson to the whole class (see page 13). Again, it is important that the teacher checks that their students understand the vocabulary that is used. Students should be encouraged to use their dictionaries to check new words.

Sentence Blocks, Discussion Questions, Role Plays, Vocabulary Tests, Verb Forms Practice

How to Use this Course

30 mins	Working in pairs or small groups, students practise the discussion questions. This is free speaking practise – the antithesis of having to make pre-set sentences using the sentence blocks. The students can change partners several times in order to get a good variety of practice, then the whole class comes together and feeds back to the group, with the teacher asking additional follow-up questions. During this time the teacher removes the sentence block sentences from the board, or asks the students to return their sentence block handouts.

We're halfway through! Have a cup of tea and some fresh air – or just hang out!

25 mins	After a relaxing break it's time for some brain work – the **lesson test** (see page 5)! The aim of this test is for the teacher to find out what vocabulary the students can remember from the previous lesson and to get an idea of how well they are coping with making the sentence blocks.
25 mins	The teacher could decide to use this slot for activities with the **discussion words** (see page 15) or for making **role plays** (see page 14) – or for both, if your students are up to the challenge!
30 mins	The students practise the sentence block sentences again, but this time without any written record – nothing on the board and no handout. The teacher monitors each pair and helps them where necessary, making sure that they are making the sentence blocks successfully. Towards the end of this time the whole class comes back together to give each other feedback. The teacher asks questions from the eight sentence blocks to different students, who should give a correct, or nearly correct, sentence – all from memory. In the early weeks this will be more difficult for the students, but after a few lessons with this method students should be able to answer confidently, having memorised some or all of that lesson's sentence blocks.
10 mins	Open question time – students can ask any English-related question. The teacher looks at the students' workbooks (this can be any suitable course book that students work through at home and which complements the lesson) and checks students' progress. The teacher sets the topic for the next lesson and gives out the handouts for the next lesson's vocabulary test. The teacher could either give or spend a few minutes eliciting the twenty new words in the students' first language. The teacher should encourage students to keep all of their handouts in their own file, for revision and further study at home.

Assessment Methods, Tests and Examination

The overall course mark for each student is reached by continuous assessment and an end of course oral examination. Individual students are monitored throughout the course and their progress recorded in a number of different ways. The aim of using continuous assessment is to encourage students to work hard in every lesson – because every lesson counts and effort is rewarded along with accuracy – and to work hard at home, e.g. learning the vocabulary words each week.

Each student gets a combined mark out of 80 for each lesson which is based on the following:

How to Use this Course

- vocabulary test: maximum of 20 marks
- lesson test: maximum of 40 marks
- student's lesson mark – accuracy: maximum of 10 marks
- student's lesson mark – effort: maximum of 10 marks

- total lesson mark: maximum of 80 marks

The lesson marks are added together on the individual Student Course Reports as the course progresses. Students don't have access to their lesson marks as they are added together, but they do see their marks for the vocabulary and lesson tests, as well as getting feedback on these tests and on their general performance each week.

Teachers should award marks out of 10 to each student for every lesson based on the level of their achievement during the lesson (accuracy) and their commitment during the lesson (effort). It goes without saying that teachers should strive to be wholly objective and not give in to favouritism when awarding these marks.

Over the ten lessons all of the lesson marks are added together to give an individual total for each student, to which is added the score from their final exam. This gives each student a grade for the whole course, ranging from A to U (ungraded fail):

- maximum lesson mark of 80 x 10 = 800 marks +
- maximum final exam mark of 100 =
- maximum course mark of 900 marks

Grade system:

Grade A = 800-900 marks   First Class
Grade B = 650-800 marks   Very Good
Grade C = 550-650 marks   Good
Grade D = 400-550 marks   Fair Pass
Grade E = 250-400 marks   Pass
Grade U = less than 250 marks   Fail

Grades A-E are passes. Grade U is ungraded and means that the student has failed the course. The student's grade is recorded on their course certificate, for example:

"Grade: A"

"Achievement: First Class"

You could use one of the course certificate templates at the back of this book (see pages 110-111), or create your own.

Lesson Assessment

During pair and group work the teacher monitors the students, checking and correcting grammar and vocabulary where necessary, e.g. during discussion question and role play

How to Use this Course

practice. In all such "free practice" work the teacher should keep referring students back to the grammar that is being learned by making the sentence blocks, for example if a student says: "What you want?", remind them that: "You must have a verb after a wh- question." In this way the free practice work will help to consolidate what is being learned from the more structured practice of forming the sentence blocks.

Written homework based on the topics and activities from each lesson could be given, checked and marked by the teacher. However, written work must be kept to a minimum during the lesson and students should not to write out full sentence blocks. This is Talk a Lot, after all! The students may instinctively begin to write down the starting sentences from the board, or make notes about the sentence blocks, but discourage this because it is a waste of lesson time in which they have a valuable opportunity to talk in English. The Talk a Lot method encourages students to use their memories as a learning tool and to activate the grammar that they already know before they join the course. **When a student writes down the sentence blocks, they give full permission to their memory to forget this information, since they know it is safely recorded somewhere**. Without the safety net of pen and paper students have to challenge themselves to work harder to make the sentence blocks (which are, after all, simply question forms and answers, based around individual verb forms). The time for writing out sentence blocks is at home, where students can write to their hearts' content! They also get a chance to see full sentence blocks in written form when they do the lesson test – once per lesson. As we have seen, the Talk a Lot certificate is based on marks gained during continuous assessment along with a final oral exam at the end of the course. Lesson assessment also includes more formal testing with regular vocabulary tests and lesson tests, the marks from which are added to each student's running total of marks. The teacher keeps track of each student's progress by adding the results of their tests and other marks to their individual Student Course Report (see page 17).

Vocabulary Tests

All Talk a Lot tests should be run in exam conditions, with folders and dictionaries closed, no talking, and no copying. The vocabulary test could be held near the beginning of the lesson, as a way of quietening students down and getting them into study mode. We recommend that the teacher runs the vocabulary and lesson tests in the same positions during the lessons each time so as to give a sense of structure and routine to the tests which can be reassuring for students. Teachers should try to mark the vocabulary test during the lesson break and give students their results in the same lesson. The teacher keeps a record of the students' scores on their Student Course Reports and measures progress made, as well as spending time during and between lessons addressing issues with individual students.

Lesson Tests

The primary aim of the regular lesson test is to consolidate the work done in the previous lesson. If you run this test immediately after the break it will help to settle students down and get their minds focused again on learning English. Set a time limit of no more than 25 minutes and stick to it. As with the vocabulary tests, the aim of the lesson test is to check students' progress and both identify weaker students who may need extra support, e.g. help with making the sentence blocks, and identify stronger students who may need a greater challenge during lessons. For example, to maximise the effect of pair work the teacher could pair a stronger student with a weaker student.

Lesson tests are marked by the teacher after the lesson and the results given to students at

How to Use this Course

the beginning of the next lesson, when there is time for a brief discussion of incorrect answers and other points raised by the test. The results from both tests enable the teacher to see not only who is paying attention during lessons, e.g. when making the sentence blocks, but also who is working at home: learning the vocabulary words, both meanings and spellings, and writing out sentence blocks.

At their discretion, a teacher may allow students who have missed a lesson to catch up on course marks by taking both tests at another time, e.g. after the present lesson. Or the teacher may decide that the student has missed the lesson and so cannot catch up on the marks, a scenario that will affect their final course score. However, if the latter applies the teacher should give the student in question the material to study at home in their own time.

Verb Forms Practice

These pages can be introduced by the teacher as extra worksheets at any time during the course if students are having problems with sentence blocks based on a particular verb form, or if they need more focused verb forms practice. A follow up activity would be for students to imagine their own sentence blocks based on particular verb forms, e.g. the teacher asks students to work in pairs and make four new sentence blocks using present perfect form – orally, without writing anything down.

In general, it's better for students to use a variety of different verb forms in a normal lesson, rather than studying a different verb form each lesson, because if a student misses one lesson they won't have missed out on studying a complete verb form.

End of Course Oral Examination

General Notes on the Examination:

The Talk a Lot end of course exam is a one to one oral examination with the teacher reading the questions and the student answering. The exam should last for a maximum of 20 minutes. The exam is recorded onto tape and marked by the teacher. The results are added to the student's individual Student Course Report and their overall course score and final grade can be calculated, which are then added to the student's certificate.

At no time should the student see the examination paper, whether before, during or after the examination. Nor should the student write down anything during the exam. The teacher writes the starting sentence and question word (printed in bold) on the board for each sentence block question.

The examination questions are taken randomly from the course work studied and include material from every topic covered during the course. During the examination the teacher should not prompt the student for answers or help them in any way, apart from to explain the instructions so that the student understands what they have to do. Students **may not** use a dictionary during this examination.

At the end of the course the teacher could give a prize to the student (or students) with:

- the best course score overall
- the best vocabulary test grades overall

How to Use this Course

- the best lesson test grades overall
- the best attendance record
- the most improved student (comparing the beginning with the end of the course)

Marking Guide:

There are four kinds of question that form the examination:

1. Make sentence blocks (questions 1, 5, 9, and 13)

The maximum score is 8 marks. Students score one mark for each fully correct line, with correct intonation and sentence stress, and one mark for naming the correct verb form. Students get only half a mark if the intonation and/or sentence stress of a line is incorrect. In the last two lines of each sentence block the answers will vary as students have to change part of the original information to produce a negative answer. Accept any answer that is grammatically correct and makes sense within the given context.

Don't penalise students for making contractions, or not making them. For example, if the answer on the examination paper says "No, he doesn't", but the student says "No, he does not", don't mark them down. It is still an accurate answer.

2. Answer discussion questions (questions 3, 6, 11 and 14)

Students can score up to a maximum of 4 points for each question based on the following criteria:

The student should answer the question and speak for approximately 1 minute:

4 marks:	the student produces sentences which are completely or almost completely correct in terms of grammar, pronunciation, intonation, and sentence stress. There are between 0-2 errors. Excellent use of vocabulary and interesting subject matter
3 marks:	the student produces sentences which are good in terms of grammar, pronunciation, intonation, and sentence stress, but there are between 3-4 errors. Good use of vocabulary
2 marks:	the student produces sentences which can be understood in terms of grammar, pronunciation, intonation, and sentence stress, but there are many errors
1 mark:	the student attempts to answer the question, but not using full sentences nor correct grammar, pronunciation, intonation, and sentence stress. Part of their answer can be clearly understood, but there are many errors
0 marks:	the student has not attempted the question or the answer is incoherent

The teacher should make a note in the box provided of several examples of the student's performance, including errors as well as correct structures.

3. State ten vocabulary words on a given topic (questions 2, 7, 12 and 15)

When students have to list ten vocabulary words, the teacher could keep a tally in the box provided, e.g. ℍℍ ℍℍ … Give a half mark in the event of wrong word stress or incorrect

How to Use this Course

intonation and/or pronunciation. When stating ten different vocabulary words the student cannot include the example word which is given in the question.

4. Answer discussion word questions (questions 4, 8, 10 and 16)

The answers and marks for these questions are provided on the examination paper. Give a half mark in the event of wrong word stress or incorrect intonation and/or pronunciation.

Sentence Blocks

Designed specifically for the Talk a Lot course, the sentence block method is a brand new way to teach English grammar with speaking practice. The main benefit of this method is that the students have to do all of the work. They must listen, think hard, and remember. They must produce eight sentences, both positive and negative, using a given verb form, and two different question forms, using wh- questions and questions with auxiliary verbs. They must produce the eight sentences based on a given starting sentence and a given wh- question word, using a pre-agreed set of rules. When they are working on the sentence blocks students are speaking and memorising correct English. They are learning to use key verb forms in English, forming questions and responses organically as they focus all their attention on making the sentence blocks successfully. They are also learning new vocabulary and have to produce their own ideas to make the last two negative sentences work.

So what is a sentence block and how do you make one? A sentence block is a group of eight consecutive sentences, made up of seven lines, that forms a two-way conversation. There are strict rules governing how a sentence block must be made, which students should learn.

At the beginning of the course:

The students receive two handouts explaining the basic terminology used when talking about sentence blocks and some helpful rules for making them (see pages 18 and 19). The teacher should spend time discussing these pages with the students, in particular explaining:

- When we use each of the eight verb forms that are explored during the course
- What we mean by subject-verb "inversion"
- How auxiliary verbs are used, and the rule for using "do" as an auxiliary verb

In the first lesson or two the teacher will need to train the students to make the seven lines that form a sentence block. In the ensuing lessons students should be able to form the sentence blocks themselves, based on the given sentences on the board or handout. It is very important that in each lesson the teacher ensures that students understand the vocabulary used in the sentence blocks before they are let loose on the task of making them.

This is an example of how an individual student could be coached to form a sentence block for the first time. When coaching groups, ask a different student for each of the lines.

The teacher has written the first starting sentence on the board; for example, this one from the "Shopping" lesson:

I used my debit card to buy a pair of shoes for work.

How to Use this Course

The teacher:
OK, we're going to make a sentence block. There are seven lines in a sentence block and eight different sentences. [Pointing to the board at the starting sentence.] This is the first line. Can you read it for me, please? [The student reads it out loud.] Do you understand this sentence?

The student:
Yes.

The teacher:
OK. [Writes "What" underneath the starting sentence.] To make the second line can you ask a "what" question based on the starting sentence?

The student:
What did you use to buy a pair of shoes for work?

The teacher:
Good. Very good. Excellent.

Note: if a student has a problem producing any part of the sentence block, the teacher should prompt them with the first word, then the next, and in this way "coax" the sentence out of them by, if necessary, saying the whole sentence and getting the student to say it with them, then to repeat it without the teacher's help.

The teacher:
And what is the short answer?

The student:
My debit card.

The teacher:
OK. Great.

Note: it is very important that the teacher praises the student as they get sentences right and gently encourages them when they have taken a wrong turn. It is also important for the teacher to keep the momentum going so that the sentence block is made with a sense of rhythm and an almost urgent pace. This will keep the student focused and thinking about the task in hand.

The teacher:
So now we've got three lines. Can you repeat them for me? [The student does so correctly.] Now, let's get to five lines. Ask a question with inversion.

The student:
Did you use your debit card to buy a pair of shoes for work?

The teacher:
Good. And the short answer?

The student:
Yes.

How to Use this Course

The teacher:
Yes, what?

The student:
Yes, I did.

The teacher:
Good. Very good. So now we've got five lines. We're almost there. Can you repeat the five lines, please? [The student does so correctly.] OK, so, to complete the sentence block, let's ask the same kind of question with inversion but this time to get a negative answer. Look at the question word. Focus on the "what". Change the "what" to get a negative answer.

The student:
Did you use cash to buy a pair of shoes for work?

The teacher:
And give a short answer in the negative.

The student:
No, I didn't.

The teacher:
Then a full negative answer. The last line is made up of two negative sentences.

The student:
I didn't use cash to buy a pair of shoes for work.

*Note: students have to invent something here ("Did you use **cash**...?") that makes sense in the same context. They should try to think of a sensible option to get a negative answer. For example, the teacher must not accept: "Did you use a car to buy a pair of shoes for work?" because it doesn't make sense. Students often struggle to remember to make two negative sentences for the last line. Encourage them and stress the two negative sentences.*

The teacher:
Excellent! Now tell me all seven lines...

Throughout, the teacher should help the student to achieve the correct pronunciation, word and sentence stress (see page 134), rhythm and intonation. If a student makes a mistake during a line, ask them to repeat the whole line again. Of course, in the example above the student has given almost all of the correct answers straight away. This is purely to serve a purpose in this guide – to give a clear example of what the students should aim for. The teacher should also encourage the students to think about word and sentence stress and to emphasise the correct words in each sentence, for example:

Did you use your **debit card** to buy a pair of shoes for work?

Yes, I **did**.

Did you use **cash** to buy a pair of shoes for work?

No, I **didn't**. I didn't use **cash** to buy a pair of shoes for work.

How to Use this Course

Students may have a tendency to try to say all seven lines with a questioning intonation at the end of each line. For example, they might say:

The student:
Did you use cash to buy a pair of shoes for work? No I didn't?

Ask them to think about the meaning of what they are saying and to make definite statements without the questioning intonation. Some students may try to gabble and deliver their lines very quickly without apparent thought of what they mean – wholly focused on their goal of remembering each line and forming the sentence blocks as quickly as possible. Ask them to slow down and to focus on what each sentence means.

So, in the example above the seven lines and eight sentences of the sentence block are:

1. I used my debit card to buy a pair of shoes for work. *(starting sentence)*

2. What did you use to buy a pair of shoes for work? *(wh- question)*

3. My debit card. *(short answer)*

4. Did you use your debit card to buy a pair of shoes for work? *(question with inversion)*

5. Yes, I did. *(short answer)*

6. Did you use cash to buy a pair of shoes for work? *(question with inversion to get a negative answer)*

7. No, I didn't. I didn't use cash to buy a pair of shoes for work. *(two sentences – a short negative answer and a long negative answer)*

The teacher should ensure that the students follow the sentence block structure and that they recap each group of sentences after the 3rd and 5th lines. If a student has a tendency to "Um…" and "Er…" their way through each line, challenge them to say the lines without doing this. As they monitor the pairs engaged in making the sentence blocks – saying one line each – the teacher will sometimes need to be firm with the students, and ask them to keep focused when it looks as though their minds are beginning to wander, and of course the teacher also needs to keep focused! For example, when leading sentence block practice at the front of the class, the teacher will need to be one step ahead of the students and know the next sentence in their mind – what they want the student to produce – before the student produces it.

Embedded Grammar:

In each lesson students will practise making positive sentences, negative sentences and question forms using the following verb forms:

- present simple
- present continuous
- past simple
- past continuous
- present perfect
- modal verbs (e.g. can, should, must, have to, etc.)
- future forms (with "will" and "going to")

Complete 12-week Spoken English Course

How to Use this Course

- first conditional

While doing sentence block practice the students may be unaware that they are using eight different verb forms. It is better not to focus on this and blow their minds with grammar, but instead make sure that the students are making the sentence blocks correctly. For example, it is essential that students understand the eight starting sentences on the board or handout at the beginning of the lesson, and also know how to make a sentence block, before they begin pair work with a partner.

The starting sentences all contain embedded grammar, which means grammar that occurs as a natural part of the sentence block as it is being spoken and automatically memorised, rather than grammar that is explicitly presented to students as an isolated grammar topic, such as: "In today's lesson we are going to study wh- questions…" etc. The embedded grammar in the sentence blocks at Elementary level includes:

- positive and negative forms
- use of articles
- use of auxiliary verbs
- a variety of main verbs in each unit
- subject and object pronouns
- yes/no questions
- wh- questions
- active and passive sentences
- punctuation marks
- prepositions of place and time
- some/any
- singular/plural
- nouns: common, proper, abstract, countable, uncountable, etc.
- intensifiers – too, really, very, completely, etc.
- use of infinitives
- adjectives
- adverbs of frequency and manner
- possessive pronouns
- determiners – this, that, those, these, etc.
- there is/there are
- formal and informal situations
- use of gerunds
- comparatives and superlatives
- relative clauses – that, which, who, where, etc.

The teacher could pick up on any or all of these grammar topics in more detail if they run the course as a 60-hour course (see page 1).

Miscellaneous Notes:

- As well as with students in groups and pairs, this method can also be used successfully with students on a one to one basis, with the teacher prompting the student to produce the sentence blocks, first with the sentences on the board or handout, and later from memory.

How to Use this Course

- Teachers (or students) can also imagine their own starting sentences based on the verb form or vocabulary that they wish to practise.

Different Ways to Practice Forming Sentence Blocks:

- In a circle – the teacher or a student leads and chooses each student in turn to form the complete sentence block.
- The students sit back to back in pairs and say one line each, then reverse who starts.
- The students chant a complete sentence block altogether as a group.
- The students say one line or one word each, going around the group in a circle.
- The teacher says a random line from a sentence block and asks a student to produce the next line.

Note: every sentence block can be said or chanted in a continuous way by adding an **eighth line** at the end that begins with "So…" and continues with the question on line 2. For example:

Line 1: Peter walks two kilometres to his office every day.
Line 2: Who walks… [etc.]
Line 7: No, he doesn't. Jeff doesn't walk two kilometres to his office every day.
Line 8: So, *who* walks… [then, continuing with line 3, "Peter does." and so on]

Discussion Questions

Students work in pairs with student A asking student B the first question, then student B asking student A the same question, before moving on to the next question. After between 5-10 minutes the students change partners and repeat the process with a different student. Where there are empty boxes on the handout – for example questions 1, 3, 4, and 6 on the Town Discussion Questions handout – the students should write down their partners' answers. This is partly to encourage the students to focus on the task in hand, and partly so that the teacher, who should be monitoring all the pairs, can see written evidence that the questions are being asked and answered. Before the students move off to work in pairs the teacher should look at the handout with the whole group and ensure that everybody understands the task and vocabulary used in the questions before they begin. For example the teacher could pre-teach some of the more difficult words and there could be a dictionary race to see which student finds each word the fastest.

Extension activity: pairs that have finished the activity early could think up their own new discussion questions based on the same topic, or the teacher could prepare additional questions for the students.

At the end of the activity the whole group comes back together for group feedback, where the teacher chooses a student to read a question and tell the class both their own answer and their partner's answer. The teacher should highlight errors that have occurred and elicit the answers from the group. Interesting structures could be explored in more detail on the board.

Assessment:

This activity is assessed by the teacher checking and correcting students as they monitor each pair, listening in and making comments where necessary, e.g. challenging incorrect question forms, and writing down notes for later exposition on the board during the group feedback period. The students' achievement in this activity is recorded as part of their overall lesson score (for accuracy and effort) by the teacher at the end of the lesson.

How to Use this Course

Role Plays

Students work in pairs or groups of three to develop and rehearse a short role play with three scenes, based on the information given to them on the handout, which is then performed to the rest of the class. They have to include the title of the outline somewhere in their role play, e.g. Family role play 1: "You did that on purpose!" The role play can be fully acted out, with props and costumes, or be simply a dialogue, but students shouldn't be writing during this activity. Writing can be done at home. In the Talk a Lot classroom the focus should be mainly on spoken English. As with the discussion questions activity the teacher should ensure that students understand what they have to do and are confident with the vocabulary used on the role play handout before they begin. The teacher should insist that each group produces three different, distinct scenes, teaching them to think of the role play as three parts of a whole, with a through-line and a logical progression through the scenes, for example:

- Scene 1: Setting up the situation
- Scene 2: Action
- Scene 3: Result

To make this task more challenging, you could agree as a group that all role plays have to include certain things, as well as what is in the outline, for example:

a) a person's name
b) a place name
c) an object (e.g. an aubergine or a giraffe's toothbrush)
d) a certain phrase
e) a prop
f) a costume

The teacher could provide a costume box and a prop box in the classroom with plenty of dressing up clothes or objects for students to use in their role plays.

If your students particularly enjoy doing role plays, they could try the role play extensions (see pages 54-56) in addition to the role play outlines on the handouts, but role play must be only one element of a Talk a Lot lesson. Make sure that in each lesson there is a balance of activities, for example: tests, sentence block building, discussion questions, role plays, etc.

It's fine when students want to veer away from the outlines given on the handouts. The aim of the activity is for the students to put the flesh on the bare bones of the outlines. For example, they should suggest character names, place names, names of businesses, and so on. The suggested outlines are only there to get ideas flowing. The teacher could suggest new situations for role plays or more imaginative groups of students could think up new role plays of their own, but based on the same lesson topic.

<u>The Mood Chart:</u>

Use the mood chart on page 57 to add an extra dimension to the role plays. Print the page onto card, cut up the cards and put them into a bag. Each student picks one card – one mood – and they have to act out their role play using this mood exclusively. When watching each role play the audience have to guess which moods the actors have picked. In another variation, the audience pick the moods that they want to see used in a role play, or all the groups have to rehearse the same role play using different moods, and the audience have to

How to Use this Course

guess the moods.

Assessment:

As with the discussion questions activity this activity is mainly assessed by the teacher checking and correcting students as they monitor the groups, listening for errors that could be dissected later on in a group feedback session, and correcting grammar in line with the work being done on forming sentence blocks. Again, the students' achievement in this activity is recorded as part of their overall lesson score (for accuracy and effort) by the teacher when they sit down and write each student's course report.

Because this activity is drama-based, the audience could make their opinion heard too, giving marks out of ten for each role play based on:

a) language accuracy
b) effort
c) imagination
d) best costumes, use of props, lighting, sound, etc.

Or they could give thumbs up (1 or 2) or thumbs down (1 or 2). The audience feedback is just for fun and not recorded on each student's course report.

Discussion Words and Question Sheets

It's amazing how much you can do with forty cut-out vocabulary words! We have outlined many activities for using these words with students on the discussion words question sheets. First of all, print a discussion words page onto thin card and cut up the cards with scissors. If possible you could laminate them to make them extra sturdy.

The main activity goes as follows: sit down with the whole class around a large table and lay out all of the cards face down. Students take a number of cards each. The number they take depends on the number of students in the class and for how long the teacher wants the activity to last, e.g. for a ten minute activity ten students could each take two cards.

Go around the group one student at a time. Each student picks up a card and has to describe the word in English without saying it. The other students have to guess the word. The students could use dictionaries to find new words that they don't know. It's possible for students to make this activity deliberately harder for their peers by giving a more cryptic description!

Using the Question Sheets:

The teacher reads the questions out loud in a random order. Or one or more of the students could read the questions out. The teacher should use as many of the questions as is necessary to fill the time that they have allotted to this activity. For example, if you have 25 minutes for this activity it's unlikely that you will need to use the main activity as described above as well as all of the questions on the handout. As with the Talk a Lot course in general, there is more material here than will probably be needed; but as all teachers know, it's better to have too much material planned for a lesson than not enough!

How to Use this Course

Extension Activities:

- The students work on the main activity with the words in pairs or small groups.

- The students have to think of ten, twenty, thirty or forty additional words on the same topic, e.g. Home, and make their own discussion words cards.

- The teacher or the students invent new questions based on the original/new words.

- Have a game of vocabulary bingo. Each student writes down fifteen words from the forty words in three lines: five on the top, five on the middle and five on the bottom. The teacher reads out words from the group at random. The students cross out the words they have written down when they hear the teacher say them. The students race to see who can cross off the first line, then two lines, then all the words.

- "Yes/No" questions: one student takes a card with a word on it, keeping it secret from the others, who have to ask "Yes/No" questions in order to find out what the word is. The first student can only answer "Yes" or "No". For example, for food and drink words the other students could ask: "Is it a vegetable?", "Is it green?", "Does it grow in a field?", etc. until they are able to guess the identity of the word. This is a great activity to get students making questions with inversion.

- The students match the phonetic and English spellings of different words (see page 142), translate words into/from the IPA, or group words by the sounds they contain.

- A student mimes different words without talking, while the others have to guess them.

- Word association activities:
  a) the teacher (or a student) chooses a word and each student has to say six words that they associate with this word, or each student in the group has to say one word. For example, if the word is "car" the students could say "wheel", "engine", "driver", "gears", "Ford", "garage", and so on.
  b) the teacher (or a student) chooses a word and the first student says the first word that comes into their head, followed by the next student and the next in a kind of word association chain. See how long your group can go for without running out of steam. You may be surprised where you end up! For example: "supermarket" > "shopping" > "centre" > "middle" > "school" > "work" > "job", and so on.

- Make any of these activities into a competition – individual or team – with points given for correct answers, and prizes. The teacher could even deduct points for incorrect answers. Prizes could be awarded for the first student to answer a question correctly, or the student who wins the vocabulary bingo, or who can think of the most new words on the same topic without a dictionary. For a fun group competition there could be a league, with the same teams competing in each lesson for points that accumulate towards a running total. It depends on how competitive your students are!

Assessment:

As with the other free practice activities in Talk a Lot (show and tell, discussion questions and role plays) assessment is performed by the teacher checking and correcting during the task, giving individual and group feedback, and referring students back to the grammar learnt from forming the sentence blocks. The students' achievement in this activity is also recorded as part of their overall lesson score (for accuracy and effort) by the teacher on each student's course report.

Sentence Blocks – Q & A

Q: What is a sentence block?

A: A sentence block is a group of eight consecutive sentences, made up of seven lines, that forms a two-way conversation. It consists of positive and negative sentences, and two question forms – a wh- question and two questions with inversion ("yes-no" questions).

Q: What is a starting sentence?

A: The first sentence in a sentence block.

Q: What is a wh- question word?

A: A question word that begins with "wh-". For example, "what", "where", "when", "who", "why", "whose", and "which". "How" is also a wh- question word because it contains the letters "h" and "w". Wh- questions are asked to obtain information, rather than a "yes" or "no" answer. They have a **falling intonation**, which means that the tone of your voice does not go up at the end of the question, as it does with "yes-no" questions.

Q: What is a question with inversion?

A: Also known as a "yes-no" question, because the answer is usually "yes" or "no", a question with inversion is a question where the subject and verb have been swapped around (or "inverted"). They always start with an auxiliary verb (be, have, or do), a modal auxiliary verb (e.g. can, will, must, should, etc.), or verb "to be". For example, this sentence is a statement: "John is a DJ". To make this statement into a question with inversion we need to swap around the verb ("is") and the subject ("John") to make: "Is John a DJ?" Questions with inversion always have a **rising intonation**, which means that the tone of your voice has to go up at the end of the question.

Q: What is an auxiliary verb?

A: Auxiliary verbs are helping verbs. They don't have any meaning of their own in the sentence, but they help the main verb to form a verb phrase. For example, in this sentence: "Ellen was talking about her sister who loves fish and chips", "was" is an auxiliary verb (from verb "to be") which works together with the main verb "talking" to make the past continuous verb form. There are three primary auxiliary verbs in English: "be", "have" and "do", as well as modal auxiliary verbs such as "can", "will" and "must".

Q: What is each of the eight verb forms used for?

A: The uses of the verb forms studied during this course can be summarised as follows:

Present Simple:	to talk about regular actions and things that are always true
Past Simple:	to talk about completed actions in the past
Present Continuous:	to talk about what is happening at the moment
Past Continuous:	to talk about continuous actions in the past: what was happening when…
Present Perfect:	to talk about past actions which are quite recent or relevant to now
Modal Verbs:	to talk about permission, possibilities, ability, and probability
Future Forms:	to talk about future plans, predictions and intentions
First Conditional:	to talk about what will happen if a certain condition is met

Sentence Blocks – Six Great Tips for Students

1. During each lesson we work with the same verb forms in the same order. Look for patterns. Each lesson try to apply what you have learnt in previous lessons.

2. After a "wh" question or phrase (such as "What time...?" or "How long...?") there <u>must</u> follow an auxiliary verb or main verb "to be".

3. Questions with inversion <u>always</u> start with an auxiliary verb or main verb "to be".

4. In questions with inversion the subject of the sentence <u>must</u> follow the auxiliary verb.

5. If there is either auxiliary verb **be** or **have** in the starting sentence, use it to make the questions and answers that follow. If there isn't, you <u>must</u> use **do** as an auxiliary verb to make the questions and answers.

6. Use as much of the starting sentence in the resulting questions and answers as you can.

Town

Sentence Blocks:

1. *(Present Simple)*   Peter walks two kilometres to his office every day.
Who

2. *(Present Continuous)*   We're waiting patiently for the bus at the bus stop opposite the church.
Where

3. *(Past Simple)*   Jennifer bought a couple of cakes at the bakery, then ran to the post office.
What

4. *(Past Continuous)*   The department store was opening until 10 o'clock because they were having a massive sale.
Why

5. *(Present Perfect)*   I've agreed to meet Dan in the old market place outside the library.
Who

6. *(Modal Verbs)*   We could drive to the lake and go fishing.
Where

7. *(Future Forms)*   The new optician's next to the bank will open next Friday.
When

8. *(First Conditional)*   If the tennis court is busy we can go to the gym instead.
What

Food and Drink

Sentence Blocks:

1. *(Present Simple)* The best kind of bread is white sliced bread.
What

2. *(Present Continuous)* Michelle is having salad and pasta because she doesn't eat meat.
Why

3. *(Past Simple)* Daniel gave himself the largest portion of ice cream.
Who

4. *(Past Continuous)* Ellen was talking about her sister who loves fish and chips.
Who

5. *(Present Perfect)* Jenny has just put the cheese in the fridge.
Where

6. *(Modal Verbs)* Potatoes can be boiled, mashed, fried, chipped, roasted or oven-baked.
How

7. *(Future Forms)* We're going to buy some fruit at the supermarket this afternoon.
When

8. *(First Conditional)* If you eat too much chocolate you will put on weight.
What

Shopping

Sentence Blocks:

1. *(Present Simple)* Emma is the manager of a small Italian restaurant.
Who

2. *(Present Continuous)* Simon is visiting the new shopping centre near St. Mark's Road.
What

3. *(Past Simple)* I used my debit card to buy a pair of shoes for work.
What

4. *(Past Continuous)* Jan was leaving the car park because she had finished her shopping.
Why

5. *(Present Perfect)* I've looked everywhere in this shop for a tin of vegetable soup, but I can't find one anywhere.
Where

6. *(Modal Verbs)* We should take the lift to the fifth floor.
What

7. *(Future Forms)* After we finish buying groceries, we'll go to Nero's for a quick coffee.
When

8. *(First Conditional)* If the checkout assistant offers to pack my bags I'll let her.
What

Health

Sentence Blocks:

1. *(Present Simple)* Being healthy is very important to me.
What

2. *(Present Continuous)* Sammi is sitting in the waiting room with her mum and brother.
Where

3. *(Past Simple)* I phoned my doctor this morning to make an appointment.
Why

4. *(Past Continuous)* Ella was telling the receptionist about her husband's painful arthritis.
Who

5. *(Present Perfect)* I've taken two tablets three times a day for a week, but I still don't feel any better.
How many

6. *(Modal Verbs)* Kenny has to take his prescription to the pharmacy tomorrow.
When

7. *(Future Forms)* Simon is going to visit the optician's for an eye examination.
Why

8. *(First Conditional)* If you ask the doctor she will give you some good advice about your problem.
What

Transport

<u>Sentence Blocks:</u>

1. *(Present Simple)*   I usually get the train at 7.28.
When

2. *(Present Continuous)*   Gemma is driving to the airport to pick up her grandmother.
Where

3. *(Past Simple)*   I flew from Heathrow to Copenhagen last night.
What

4. *(Past Continuous)*   Oliver was crossing the road when he was hit by a bus.
Who

5. *(Present Perfect)*   We've cancelled our flight because our daughter is ill.
Why

6. *(Modal Verbs)*   All passengers must show their passports and boarding passes at the gate.
What

7. *(Future Forms)*   The next train to arrive at platform 8 will be the 9.49 service to Cardiff.
Which

8. *(First Conditional)*   If we cycle to work we'll get there in about an hour.
When

Family

Sentence Blocks:

1. *(Present Simple)* My mum lives with her new partner in Brighton.
Where

2. *(Present Continuous)* Roberto's daughter is playing with her cousins.
What

3. *(Past Simple)* Jenna's aunt and uncle visited us in May because they wanted to see our new baby.
Why

4. *(Past Continuous)* My sister was walking to the city museum with her children when she saw a fox.
Where

5. *(Present Perfect)* The whole family has decided to go on holiday to Florida next year.
Who

6. *(Modal Verbs)* Your grandma and granddad should think about moving into a retirement bungalow.
Whose

7. *(Future Forms)* Sam's brother is going to start university in Edinburgh next September.
When

8. *(First Conditional)* If our parents get divorced the family will be very disappointed.
What

Clothes

Sentence Blocks:

1. *(Present Simple)* I wear glasses because I'm short-sighted.
Why

2. *(Present Continuous)* Harry is trying on a new pair of smart black trousers.
Who

3. *(Past Simple)* Frankie bought herself a new dress and some underwear in the trendiest boutique on Oxford Street.
Where

4. *(Past Continuous)* Michael was wearing the yellow and brown striped pyjamas that his grandma had knitted him for Christmas.
Who

5. *(Present Perfect)* I have always liked jackets and tops from Marks and Spencer.
What

6. *(Modal Verbs)* Stephen has to wear a blue and grey uniform every day for his job as a security guard.
When

7. *(Future Forms)* We'll have a clearout of our wardrobe to see what we can give away to charity.
Why

8. *(First Conditional)* If you wear a suit and tie to the interview you'll make an excellent impression.
What kind

Work

Sentence Blocks:

1. *(Present Simple)* Gerry hates working part-time for his dad's furniture business.
Who

2. *(Present Continuous)* Helena is hoping to get promoted at the end of the year.
When

3. *(Past Simple)* When Greg worked for Dell he had to do plenty of overtime.
What

4. *(Past Continuous)* Edward was updating his CV because he wanted to apply for a new job.
Why

5. *(Present Perfect)* My friend Jo has been unemployed since last August.
How long

6. *(Modal Verbs)* You need to ask your manager for a pay rise as soon as possible!
What

7. *(Future Forms)* I'm going to visit that new employment agency about temporary work.
Where

8. *(First Conditional)* Dave will have to work very hard if he wants to have a successful career in sales.
What

Home

Sentence Blocks:

1. *(Present Simple)* I live in a small semi-detached house in Manchester.
Where

2. *(Present Continuous)* Mark is buying a new washing machine because his old one is broken.
Why

3. *(Past Simple)* When I went to their home Jack and Lisa showed me their new bathroom.
What

4. *(Past Continuous)* Sarah and Noel were watching funny DVDs in their living room for three hours last night.
Who

5. *(Present Perfect)* Jason has finished cutting the grass in the back garden.
What

6. *(Modal Verbs)* Barry has to do the washing up every night after tea.
How often

7. *(Future Forms)* I'll do the hoovering quickly before I have a bath.
When

8. *(First Conditional)* If you sell your horrible flat you'll be able to put down a deposit on a nice house.
What

Free Time

Sentence Blocks:

1. *(Present Simple)* I love going to the cinema with my friends, because we always have a good time.
Why

2. *(Present Continuous)* Barney and Wanda are enjoying a day out at an amusement park.
Who

3. *(Past Simple)* We went on a camping holiday last summer for two weeks.
How long

4. *(Past Continuous)* Chester's son was playing golf badly yesterday afternoon with a few friends from his cousin's bowling club.
How

5. *(Present Perfect)* I have seen Macbeth at this theatre five times.
How many

6. *(Modal Verbs)* You should do some exercise instead of playing computer games all day.
What

7. *(Future Forms)* Me, Jess and Casey are going to watch the tennis in the park.
Where

8. *(First Conditional)* If the leisure centre is still open we can all go swimming.
What

Sentence Block Extensions

------------------------------✂------------------------------

Town:

Make new sentence blocks from the starting sentences in this lesson using different "wh-" question words:

	WHAT	**WHERE**	**WHEN**	**WHO**	**WHY**	**WHICH**	**HOW**
1.	what	where	when				how far
2.				who	why	which	how
3.	what (2nd)	where (x2)		who			how
4.	what, what time		when			which	
5.	what	where					
6.	what (x2)						how
7.	what	where				which	
8.	what (2nd)	where	when				

------------------------------✂------------------------------

Food & Drink:

Make new sentence blocks from the starting sentences in this lesson using different "wh-" question words:

	WHAT	**WHERE**	**WHEN**	**WHO**	**WHY**	**WHICH**	**HOW**
1.						which	
2.	what			who			
3.	what					which	
4.	what					which	
5.	what			who			
6.	what						
7.	what	where		who			
8.							how

------------------------------✂------------------------------

Shopping:

Make new sentence blocks from the starting sentences in this lesson using different "wh-" question words:

	WHAT	**WHERE**	**WHEN**	**WHO**	**WHY**	**WHICH**	**HOW**
1.	what, what kind						
2.		where		who		which	
3.	what (2nd)				why		
4.	what (x2)	where		who			
5.	what						
6.		where		who		which	
7.	what (x2)	where		who			
8.				who			

------------------------------✂------------------------------

Sentence Block Extensions

--✂--

Health:

Make new sentence blocks from the starting sentences in this lesson using different "wh-" question words:

	WHAT	WHERE	WHEN	WHO	WHY	WHICH	HOW
1.							how
2.	what			who (x2)			
3.	what		when	who, whose			
4.	what			who (2nd), whose			
5.	what						how, how long
6.	what (x2)	where		who			
7.	what	where		who			
8.	what (2nd)			who			

--✂--

Transport:

Make new sentence blocks from the starting sentences in this lesson using different "wh-" question words:

	WHAT	WHERE	WHEN	WHO	WHY	WHICH	HOW
1.	what (x2), what time						
2.	what	where		who (x2)	why		how
3.		where (x2)	when			which (x2)	how
4.	what		when				
5.	what			who			
6.		where	when	who			
7.	what (x4: train, time, platform, destination)					which (2nd)	
8.	what						

--✂--

Family:

Make new sentence blocks from the starting sentences in this lesson using different "wh-" question words:

	WHAT	WHERE	WHEN	WHO	WHY	WHICH	HOW
1.				who (x2), whose			
2.				who (x2), whose (x2)			
3.			when	who (x2), whose			
4.	what (x2)		when	who (x2), whose (x2)		which	
5.	what	where	when				how many
6.	what	where		who			
7.	what	where		who, whose		which	
8.			when	who	why		how

--✂--

Sentence Block Extensions

Clothes:

Make new sentence blocks from the starting sentences in this lesson using different "wh-" question words:

	WHAT	WHERE	WHEN	WHO	WHY	WHICH	HOW
1.	what						
2.	what (x2), what kind						
3.	what			who			
4.	what					which	
5.	what						how long
6.	what, what colour			who	why	which	
7.	what (x2)			who			
8.	what						

Work:

Make new sentence blocks from the starting sentences in this lesson using different "wh-" question words:

	WHAT	WHERE	WHEN	WHO	WHY	WHICH	HOW
1.	what (x2)					which	
2.	what			who			
3.			when	who			
4.	what (x2)			who			
5.	who						
6.	what (2nd)		when	who			
7.	what (x2)			who	why	which	
8.				who			

Home:

Make new sentence blocks from the starting sentences in this lesson using different "wh-" question words:

	WHAT	WHERE	WHEN	WHO	WHY	WHICH	HOW
1.	what kind						
2.	what			who			
3.			when	who			
4.	what (x2)		when				how long
5.	what (2nd)	where		who		which	
6.	what		when	who			
7.	what						how
8.	what (2nd)		when				how

Sentence Block Extensions

Free Time:

Make new sentence blocks from the starting sentences in this lesson using different "wh-" question words:

	WHAT	WHERE	WHEN	WHO	WHY	WHICH	HOW
1.	what	where		who			
2.	what (x2)	where					
3.	what (x2)	where	when				
4.	what		when	who (x2)			how many
5.	what	where					
6.				who			
7.	what (x2)			who			
8.			when	who			

Town

Discussion Questions:

1. Do you live in a town or a city?

Tell me more about where you live.

2. What do you like about where you live? What don't you like? How could it be improved?

3. Who is in charge of your town or city?

Do you think they do a good job? Do you vote in local elections?

4. What are the best things to see and do in your town or city?

5. Describe your journey from home to work or school.

6. If you could live anywhere in the world, where would you live and why?

7. What are the main problems in your town or city (e.g. crime, vandalism, homelessness, drugs, graffiti, etc.)? What is being done about them? How can you help?

8. Have you ever lived abroad? Talk about your favourite towns or cities abroad (or in this country).

Food and Drink

Discussion Questions:

1. What is your favourite food? [ ]

Why do you like it? How often do you eat it? What is your favourite drink? Why?

2. What is your least favourite food? [ ]

Why don't you like it? What is your least favourite drink? Why?

3. Where do you shop for food and drink? [ ]

Do you enjoy food shopping? How long does it take you normally?

4. What do you think about vegetarians? Are you a vegetarian, or do you know anyone who is? What do you / they eat?

5. What do you eat for… a) breakfast, b) lunch, c) dinner, d) a snack?

6. Are you hungry? [ ] Are you thirsty? [ ]

When did you last eat and drink?

7. Do you watch cookery programmes on TV? What do you think of them? Have you ever followed a recipe from one of them? Tell me more.

8. Who is your favourite film star? [ ]

If they asked you to make them a sandwich, what would you put in it? Why?

[ ]

Shopping

Discussion Questions:

1. Do you enjoy shopping? ☐ Why? / Why not?

2. How often do you buy clothes? ☐

How much do you usually spend on… a) clothes, b) shoes, c) jewellery?

3. Who do you usually go shopping with? ☐

4. What are your favourite shops? ☐

Why? Which shops do you never go in? Why not?

5. Have you ever worked in a shop? Tell me about it.

6. Have you ever asked for a refund? What happened? How did you feel? Have you ever bought something that you really regretted?

7. When did you last buy something nice for yourself? What was it and how expensive was it?

☐

8. Do you shop online? ☐ If yes, how often do you shop online?

What do you buy? Which websites would you recommend?

Health

Discussion Questions:

1. Have you ever been to hospital? ▢ Tell me about it.

2. What would you do if a member of your family, or your best friend, had an accident?

3. How healthy are you? How often do you get ill? Do you go to the gym or exercise regularly?

4. What is the name, address and phone number of your dentist?

▢

5. Do you know anyone who is a hypochondriac? Are you one? Tell me more.

6. How would you make an appointment with your doctor – in English?

▢

7. Do you take vitamin supplements or natural remedies? ▢

Do they have any effect?

8. Who is the unhealthiest person you know? ▢

Have you tried to encourage them to be healthier? Tell me more.

Transport

Discussion Questions:

1. What is your favourite mode of transport? Why?

What is your least favourite mode of transport? Why?

2. Can you drive? Tell me about learning to drive (or why you can't drive).

3. If you had the choice, where in the world would you visit that you haven't visited before? Why? Who would you take with you? How long would you go for?

4. Can you ride a bike? Tell me about learning to ride a bike (or why you can't ride a bike).

5. Tell me about a terrible journey that you've taken, e.g. you had one of these problems: cancellation / accident / lost luggage, etc.

6. What is the biggest problem with public transport in your town or city?

7. How do you think transport will be different from now in fifty years' time?

8. Would you like to fly in a space shuttle? Why? / Why not? How would you feel if you had this opportunity?

Family

Discussion Questions:

1. Tell me about your family...

2. Is there anyone in your family that you don't like or don't get on with? Why not?

3. Who is the funniest member of your family? Why?

4. Have you ever lived far away from your family? Would you like to in the future? How did / would you feel?

5. Do you have children? Tell me about them. If not, would you like to have children in the future? Why? / Why not?

6. Which member of your family are you closest to? Why?

7. Have you ever tried to make your family tree? Tell me about it. If not, would you like to start making one? Why? / Why not?

8. How important is your family to you? Are families important to society? Why? / Why not? What would society be like without families?

Clothes

Discussion Questions:

1. What is your favourite item of clothing? [ ]

Why do you like it? Where did you get it from? How long have you had it?

2. Which item of clothing do you hate the most? [ ]

Why? When are you going to get rid of it?

3. What do you wear to feel: a) smart, b) comfortable, c) fun?

[a)]   [b)]   [c)]

4. Have you ever bought something, worn it once, then taken it back to the shop for a refund? What happened?

5. Who is the best dressed / worst dressed person…

a) in the public eye [ ]

b) that you know [ ]

6. If you were given £3,000 to spend only on clothes and shoes, what would you buy and where would you go shopping?

7. Do you follow fashion? Who and what is in / out of fashion at the moment? Have you ever been to a fashion show? Describe what happened.

8. Where do you usually shop for clothes and shoes? What are the best shops in your town or city? Have you ever shopped online for clothes or shoes? Do you ever buy second-hand clothes or shoes?

Work

Discussion Questions:

1. What is your job at the moment?

Tell me about it. What do you like about it? What don't you like?

2. Tell me about the best and worst jobs that you have ever had.

The best...   *The worst...*

3. If you could do any job in the world what would it be?

Why?

4. Who do you think has got the easiest / hardest job in the world? Why?

5. If you won £10 million on the lottery, would you still go to work? Why? / Why not? If you didn't have to work, what would you do every day?

6. Who is the laziest person at your workplace?

Do you think that they should get the sack? Why? / Why not?

7. Have you or somebody you know ever been unemployed?

How did you / they feel? How did you / they find a job? What other ways are there to find a job?

8. Is it harder to be a manager than an employee? Why? / Why not?

Home

Discussion Questions:

1. Do you live in a house, flat or bungalow? Describe where you live. Now describe it in three words: ☐

2. Describe your dream home. Where would you like to live if you could live anywhere? Talk about location, type of home, number of rooms, furniture, swimming pool, garden, staff, etc.

3. Do you have a garden? ☐ Do you enjoy gardening? ☐ Why? / Why not?

4. What would you do if you lost your home and became homeless? What are some of the reasons that people become homeless?

5. If there was a fire at your home, what would you rescue first? Why?

☐

6. Is your home tidy or messy? How tidy is it on a scale of 1=very messy to 10=very tidy? How often do you clean your home? Describe what you do. Do you have any friends with either very messy or very tidy homes?

7. What is your favourite room in your home? ☐ Why? How much time do you spend there? What do you do there?

8. What are your neighbours like? Describe them. Do you get on well with them? Why? / Why not?

Free Time

Discussion Questions:

1. How much free time do you have? When do you usually have free time?

2. What sports do you enjoy watching or playing?

What sports would you like to try that you haven't tried yet? What sports would you *never* try?

3. Tell me about a memorable holiday. Where was it? Who did you go with? Why did you decide to go there? What happened?

4. Do you enjoy going on scary rides at amusement parks? Why? / Why not?

5. How often do you go to the cinema / theatre? What is your favourite film / play…?

6. Do you like reading? What do you read? Tell me about your favourite newspaper / magazine / book / website…

7. Describe a typical weekend. What do you do?

8. Do you regularly surf the 'net or play computer or video games? Tell me more. If you don't, why not?

Town

Role Plays:

1. "Water and books do not mix!"

Place: Your local library
Time: 5pm
Characters: You and a librarian
Situation: You are returning a book about water-skiing that you borrowed for a recent holiday. Unfortunately the book has been damaged because you were reading it *whilst* water-skiing

Scenes: i) You try to return the book when the librarian is not looking
ii) You have to explain to the librarian why the book is damaged and *who* damaged it (you can be an imaginative liar!)
iii) The librarian goes to ask a senior librarian for advice about how much you should be charged for the damage, then returns

If there are three people in the group the third character could be:

a) The senior librarian
b) Somebody reading at the library who says "Sshh! I'm trying to read!" quite a lot
c) The author of the book

2. "Excuse me, where is the train station…?"

Place: The market place in your town
Time: 2 o'clock in the afternoon
Characters: You and a foreign tourist
Situation: A foreign tourist stops you to ask for directions to the train station. They don't speak English very well

Scenes: i) The tourist asks you for directions to the train station. You don't understand them well, but give them directions to the Tourist Information Centre, where they can get a map of the town
ii) Later in the afternoon: you meet the tourist again. They can't find the Tourist Information Centre. You agree to go there with them
iii) At the Tourist Information Centre you ask for train times for the tourist, but unfortunately they have now missed their train

If there are three people in the group the third character could be:

a) Someone who works at the Tourist Information Centre
b) The tourist's friend or partner
c) The mayor of your town

Complete 12-week Spoken English Course

Food and Drink

Role Plays:

1. "Waiter, there's a mouse in my potato!"

Place: Le Maison Souris – an exclusive French restaurant
Time: 8pm
Characters: You and a waiter
Situation: You are having dinner at Le Maison Souris

Scenes:
i) During the starter you find a human hair in your soup
ii) During the main course you discover a dead mouse in your mashed potatoes
iii) During the dessert you find a gold necklace in your ice cream

If there are three people in the group the third character could be:

a) Your friend or partner who is also at the meal
b) The manager of the restaurant
c) Another customer dining at a different table
d) The waiter's friend or aged parent

2. "Have you ever driven a camel before?"

Place: A very hot desert in the middle of nowhere
Time: 12 noon – the hottest part of the day
Characters: You and a camel driver
Situation: You are a famous explorer who is lost in the desert. You desperately need to find water or you will die. The camel driver is trying to get fifty camels to the market of the nearest town, which is 10 miles away

Scenes:
i) You agree to help the camel driver in return for water
ii) During the journey some of the camels refuse to move
iii) At the end of the journey you try to buy two of the camels from the camel driver to help you continue your travels

If there are three people in the group the third character could be:

a) The camel driver's lazy assistant
b) Your long-lost adopted brother or sister
c) A reluctant camel
d) An unscrupulous market trader

Shopping

Role Plays:

1. "That's not my DVD player!"

Place: A shop that sells electrical goods
Time: 4pm
Characters: You and a sales assistant
Situation: Last Saturday you bought a new DVD player from the shop. When you opened the box you discovered that the player was a completely different model from the one on the box – a much cheaper one. You would like a full refund and an apology

Scenes: i) You ask for a refund. The sales assistant tries to deal with the problem but only the manager can authorise a refund. The sales assistant says that they have gone out but will be back at 5 o'clock
ii) It's 5 o'clock. You return to the shop but there is no sign of the manager. You are getting angry and decide to take a DVD player from the stock room – the model that you should have had
iii) The manager returns

If there are three people in the group the third character could be:

a) Another difficult customer in the shop
b) A police officer
c) Your elderly grandmother

2. "Extra! Extra! Read all about it!"

Place: A street in your town
Time: 11.30am
Characters: You and a newspaper seller
Situation: You buy a newspaper from a small kiosk on the street. The seller gives you the wrong change for a five pound note

Scenes: i) You buy the newspaper and discover the mistake
ii) You challenge the seller but they refuse to accept that they have made a mistake
iii) You decide to set up your own newspaper kiosk next to the seller's and start a price war by selling your newspapers at a discount

If there are three people in the group the third character could be:

a) Somebody buying a newspaper from you
b) Your annoying sister-in-law or uncle
c) A teenager trying to buy cigarettes for his under-age friends

Health

Role Plays:

1. "But I must see my doctor now!"

Place: Your local family doctor's surgery
Time: 10am
Characters: You and the doctor's receptionist
Situation: You need to make an appointment for today to see your doctor because you've got a very bad cold. You want to see the doctor now because at 10.30am you are going bowling, then having a haircut, then having a sauna, and then having a romantic meal – all with different people

Scenes:
i) You ask to see the doctor now, but there are no appointments until this afternoon
ii) You phone your various friends to try to rearrange your day, but it's not possible
iii) You fake a coughing fit and the receptionist has to decide whether to let you see the doctor now as an emergency, or stick to surgery policy...

If there are three people in the group the third character could be:

a) One or more of your different friends on the phone
b) Your doctor
c) Another patient in the waiting room – someone with a more serious problem – who has been waiting to see the doctor much longer than you

2. "It shouldn't cost the earth to keep fit!"

Place: Your local gym
Time: 3pm
Characters: You and the gym manager
Situation: You want to keep fit and lose weight, but you don't want to pay the high prices charged by the gym

Scenes:
i) You speak to the manager about a discount. You say that you are a DJ on a local radio station and can give the gym good publicity for free if they give you some money off the monthly fee
ii) The manager agrees to give you a free session at the gym today, and then talk about the discount later. You enjoy using the equipment at the gym
iii) Unfortunately you break one of the running machines because you are too heavy for it. The manager has to decide whether to make a deal with you or not – and what about the cost of the broken machine?

If there are three people in the group the third character could be:

a) Somebody else using the gym who also would like a discount on the monthly fee
b) The manager's area manager, who overhears the first conversation and is not happy

Transport

Role Plays:

1. "That's not music – it's just noise!"

Place: You are on a bus going to work
Time: 8.15am
Characters: You and a teenager
Situation: You are on a crowded bus on the way to work. You have to stand because the bus is full. A teenager starts playing loud rap music from the speaker on their mobile phone, to impress their cool friends. Some people on the bus find this annoying

Scenes: i) You ask the teenager to turn the music down or off. They refuse
              ii) You ask the bus driver to talk to the teenager about the music and how it is disturbing you and the other paying passengers. The driver is afraid of the teenagers and says that he can't hear the music
              iii) You take matters into your own hands and confront the teenager again. You take the phone and the teenager gets very angry

If there are three people in the group the third character could be:

   a) *The bus driver*
   b) *One of the teenager's cool friends*
   c) *An off-duty bouncer from a local nightclub who gets involved*

2. "I wanted a return ticket to Birmingham!"

Place: The coach station in your town
Time: 2.45pm
Characters: You and a customer service assistant
Situation: You would like to find out the times of coaches to Birmingham this evening and buy a return ticket. You want to come home tomorrow afternoon

Scenes: i) You go to the ticket counter and tell the customer service assistant what you want. They find the times for you, print your tickets and you pay them with your debit card
              ii) After you have left the counter, you realise that the tickets are wrong. They have given you a return ticket to Manchester, coming back next Friday morning at 4 o'clock
              iii) You go back to the counter, but find a long queue. You go straight to the front and try to talk to the assistant, but they won't serve you unless you go to the back of the queue – even though it was their mistake

If there are three people in the group the third character could be:

   a) *The customer service assistant's supervisor*
   b) *Somebody else waiting in the queue*

Complete 12-week Spoken English Course

Family

Role Plays:

1. "You did that on purpose!"

Place: Your cousin's wedding
Time: 2.35pm
Characters: You and the bride-to-be
Situation: With the wedding due to start at 3pm you are talking to your cousin's bride-to-be, trying to calm her down because she is very nervous. She was your girlfriend ten years ago in high school but you are over her now

Scenes: i) The bride makes you laugh and you accidentally spill your glass of red wine all over her dress
ii) You try to clean up the dress. The bride-to-be is in tears and very angry. She accuses you of being jealous that she is getting married to your cousin and says that you ruined her dress on purpose
iii) After a moment, you and the bride-to-be realise that you are still madly in love with each other. Will the wedding be cancelled?

If there are three people in the group the third character could be:

a) Your cousin
b) The mother of the bride-to-be

2. "A mean man whose wallet rarely opened!"

Place: The funeral of your late Uncle Charles
Time: 2.30pm
Characters: You and Charles Jnr. – Uncle Charles's son
Situation: You have been chosen to read a speech at your uncle's funeral. All of your family are there. They are all upset because Uncle Charles was much loved and will be greatly missed. You have just flown in from Fiji for the funeral and have been very busy with work lately, so you let your cousin, Charles Jnr., write the speech for you

Scenes: i) Before the funeral Charles Jnr. gives you the speech moments before the funeral begins. You don't have time to read it before going up to the front
ii) You read out the speech but as you do so it becomes clear, from the offensive language used in it, that Charles Jnr. hated his father because he had excluded him from his will. You see that the family are very offended by the speech and that your life may now be in danger
iii) Later on you confront Charles Jnr., who explains why he wrote the speech

If there are three people in the group the third character could be:

a) A family member at the funeral, who is horrified by the speech
b) Auntie Gladys – Uncle Charles's wife

Sentence Blocks, Discussion Questions, Role Plays, Vocabulary Tests, Verb Forms Practice

Clothes

Role Plays:

1. "Can I just try this on again?"

Place:	A clothes shop in your town
Time:	9.30am
Characters:	You and a sales assistant
Situation:	You need to find an outfit for a friend's engagement party

Scenes:
i) You are not sure what colour, style, or size outfit you want, so you ask the sales assistant to bring several different options
ii) You try on outfit after outfit. There is something wrong with all of them. The sales assistant has to go back and forth between the shop and the changing room several times until they are absolutely fed up
iii) You decide to buy the first outfit that you tried on. The sales assistant tells you what they think of your decision

If there are three people in the group the third character could be:

a) *Another customer who is waiting to be served*
b) *Your friend who keeps giving you advice about the clothes, which makes you even more confused*
c) *The manager of the shop who is annoyed that the sales assistant isn't serving the other customers*

2. "No – *you* go home and change!"

Place:	Your partner's birthday party
Time:	8.15pm
Characters:	You and a former friend that you don't get on with
Situation:	You have splashed out on a whole new outfit for this very special occasion

Scenes:
i) Your former friend arrives at the party wearing exactly the same outfit as you. They think that you should go home and change, whilst you think that they should do the same. In the end you both decide to change
ii) Later on. You both arrive at the party wearing a different outfit, but still exactly the same outfit as each other. You both go home to change
iii) Much later on. You arrive at the party wearing the first outfit again. Moments later your former friend arrives, also wearing the first outfit

If there are three people in the group the third character could be:

a) *Your partner, whose birthday party it is*
b) *Somebody else at the party who is wearing exactly the same outfit as well*
c) *An over-enthusiastic party DJ*

Work

Role Plays:

1. "This company's not made of money!"

Place: Your boss's office
Time: 10.44am
Characters: You and your boss
Situation: You haven't had a pay rise for two years. You work hard and do plenty of overtime, so after a lot of thought you decide to pluck up courage to ask your boss for a pay rise

Scenes:
i) You ask your boss for a pay rise. They don't make a decision but ask you to come back at 4pm with a list of ten good reasons why they should give you a pay rise
ii) It's 4pm and you return to see your boss. You read out your list but they still don't want to give you a pay rise. In fact, they ask you to do more overtime
iii) One hour later you are in the lift going to the ground floor. Your boss gets in as well, eating a salmon baguette. You are alone together. Suddenly they begin choking on a piece of salmon. Do you help?

If there are three people in the group the third character could be:

a) Your boss's secretary
b) A colleague at work who doesn't like you and also wants a pay rise

2. "How could you do a thing like that?"

Place: The staff canteen at your workplace
Time: 5.40pm
Characters: You and a work colleague
Situation: At the end of a very long day you go into the staff canteen to get your sandwich box from the fridge

Scenes:
i) You witness a colleague stealing money from the employees' holiday fund tin. You know that they have got financial problems at home. They don't know that you saw them
ii) The next day everybody is talking about who could have stolen £45 from the holiday fund. You ask your colleague about it, but they say that they don't know anything about it. You tell them that you're there if they ever need to talk
iii) Your colleague comes to you and confesses. You both go to explain to your boss what happened

If there are three people in the group the third character could be:

a) Your boss
b) Another colleague, who is sure that *you* stole the money

Home

<u>Role Plays:</u>

1. "This could be 'Your Best Move' yet!"

Place:	"Your Best Move" – an estate agent's office in London
Time:	2.30pm
Characters:	You and an estate agent
Situation:	You are looking for a small semi-detached house in a quiet suburb, but the estate agent wants to sell you a smart expensive apartment in the centre of London
Scenes:	i) In the estate agent's you arrange to view both the house and the apartment ii) The viewing of the house iii) The viewing of the apartment and your decision about both properties

If there are three people in the group the third character could be:

a) *Your friend or partner*
b) *The manager of the estate agent's*
c) *The present owner of the house or apartment*
d) *A homeless person*

2. "Just tidy up – or else!"

Place:	Your home
Time:	1.30pm
Characters:	Two people who live together, e.g. friends, flatmates or partners
Situation:	One of you is a very tidy person and one of you is very messy. The tidy person wants the messy one to help out more at home and try to keep their home nice and clean
Scenes:	i) A big row: the tidy person tells the messy person to clean the house – or else! Then they go out leaving the messy person alone at home ii) The messy person decides to either tidy up and start cleaning, or do something more interesting, like watch TV or chat to friends on the phone iii) The tidy person comes home and finds out whether their home is clean or not. They either reward or punish the messy person depending on their work

If there are three people in the group the third character could be:

a) *Another tidy or messy friend / flatmate who lives there too*
b) *A nosy window cleaner*
c) *A timid door to door salesman who is trying to sell life insurance*

Free Time

Role Plays:

1. "Sssshhhh!"

Place: Your local cinema
Time: 9.40pm
Characters: You and the person sitting in front of you
Situation: You are with friends at the cinema, waiting for the film to start

Scenes:
i) The film begins. The person sitting in front of you is eating popcorn so loudly that it is difficult for you to hear the film. You complain and they agree to eat more quietly
ii) A few minutes later their friend arrives late. They are very tall and sit in the seat directly in front of you, so that you can't see the screen very well. You complain again and the friend agrees to sit further down in their seat
iii) Half an hour later the person sitting in front of you is chatting on their mobile. You complain for the third time and they ask you if you want to "take it outside"…

If there are three people in the group the third character could be:

a) The tall friend
b) One of your friends
c) A cinema employee, or the cinema manager

2. "I'll get you for this!"

Place: On a ski slope in the Alps
Time: 11.20am
Characters: You and another skier
Situation: You are a novice skier having lessons

Scenes:
i) Whilst practising your skiing you accidentally run into somebody and break their leg
ii) At the hospital you apologise for the accident, but they want to take you to court to sue you for loss of income because they are a world famous dancer and were about to star in a West End musical in London. You try to talk your way out of it and leave a false name and address
iii) One year later you are at the same skiing resort. By chance you meet the dancer again and both laugh about what happened. You slap them on the back in a friendly way, but they lose their balance and fall down the slope backwards. They end up back in hospital, this time with *both* legs broken

If there are three people in the group the third character could be:

a) The other skier's partner or agent
b) The other skier's lawyer

Role Play Extensions

Here are some additional situations for students to use as starting points for new role plays:

--✂--

Town:

1. At the bank: you want to take out a loan, but you have a low credit, rating so you have to try a few different banks / loan companies / loan sharks…

2. At school / college / university: you organise a field trip. On the coach you have to take charge when several students are sick. Then you are accused of stealing money from the trip fund. Did you steal it…?

--✂--

Food & Drink:

1. At a sandwich shop: it's your job to make the sandwiches, but you are very tired from a late night out and customers keep coming in to ask for more and more exotic sandwich fillings. You have to find the ingredients, or improvise with what you have…

2. In a pub: it's your 18th birthday and you are trying to get your first pint of beer from a landlord who becomes suspicious because of your youthful appearance…

--✂--

Shopping:

1. At a supermarket checkout: you want to pay for your shopping (two tins of beans) but all you have is a £20 note. There is a long queue behind you and the checkout assistant won't accept your cash because they haven't got enough change…

2. In the butcher's / bakery / greengrocer's / any shop: first, you can't find any sausages / rolls / pears / etc. Next, the sales assistant scans your shopping but you notice that they scan a few items twice by accident…

--✂--

Health:

1. At your dentist's: you make an appointment to have a tooth out. Your dentist is very chatty but it's hard to reply with your mouth full of instruments. Afterwards you discover that they have taken out the wrong tooth…

2. At a pharmacy: you need some sachets of cold relief powder. You want blackcurrant flavour, but all they have on display are lemon flavoured ones. The sales assistant is reluctant to go and check whether they have any blackcurrant flavoured sachets…

--✂--

Role Play Extensions

--✂--

Transport:

1. On the street: you are cycling to work when a car runs into you. You are OK, but your new bike is broken beyond repair. The driver refuses to accept responsibility for the accident, even though it was their fault…

2. In a taxi: you are on a long journey with a very boring taxi driver who tells you endless stories about the celebrities that he has had in the back of his cab. To stop him from boring you to death, you tell him that you are also a celebrity – in Belgium – and make up stories about why you are famous…

--✂--

Family:

1. At a family reunion: first, you find that you don't recognise many of the people there because you haven't seen them for so long; you end up getting lots of their names wrong. Then, you are surprised when you meet your uncle's new wife, who is the same age as you, i.e. less than half his age…

2. It's Christmas Day: first, you don't get the presents that you wanted; then, you have to break up a fight between your niece and nephew over who gets to play on the new games console…

--✂--

Clothes:

1. At home: you agree to give away some of your old clothes to charity. Your partner or roommate gets to work sorting them out and, without your knowledge, gives away some of your very best clothes…

2. At work: you have to wear a new uniform, but you hate it – both the design and the colour. It makes you look awful. You try different ways of improving it, much to the annoyance of your manager…

--✂--

Work:

1. At work: it's your first day in a new job. You accidentally break a valuable vase in your boss's office. You try to cover up what happened but the office gossip hears about it…

2. At the careers adviser's office: you discuss your CV and skills with the careers adviser. They decide that you should apply for a boring office job and tell you to apply for four jobs that they find online. However, you have always had a burning ambition to become a professional wrestler…

--✂--

Role Play Extensions

--✂--

Home:

1. On your driveway at home: you are washing your car, when you find a scratch and a small dent on the side. You confront your son or daughter, who borrowed the car last night to go to a party, but they are hiding somewhere in the house. You have to look in every room…

2. At home: you have just moved into a new flat and you throw a fantastic flat-warming party to celebrate. It's interrupted halfway-through when the person who lives downstairs bangs on the door and asks you to turn down the music…

--✂--

Free Time:

1. At a football match: you are in a large crowd at a match between City and United. You are supporting your beloved City but it seems that you are in the wrong part of the stadium and everybody around you is passionately supporting United…

2. At a travel agent's: you are trying to decide on a holiday destination but your friend or partner just can't make up their mind…

--✂--

Role Plays – Mood Chart

I'm feeling…

nosey	bored	sad	cheerful
angry	happy	shocked	up
frightened	smug	apologetic	secretive
down	worried	so so	aggressive
guilty	ecstatic	paranoid	naughty
surprised	energetic	friendly	unwell
depressed	moody	determined	tired
giggly	upset	mischievous	disgusted
too hot	excited	cold	nervous
stupid	horrified	relieved	confused

Town

Discussion Words:

pavement	bed and breakfast	office	bakery
apartment block	bank	church	bookshop
bus stop	optician's	building site	mosque
clothes shop	football stadium	post office	casino
library	river	tennis court	school
community centre	building	cathedral	traffic lights
department store	market place	chemist	university
college	town	car showroom	village
town hall	lake	bridge	police station
holiday resort	public toilets	city	tax office

Town

General Questions:

1. Are there any words that you don't know? Use a dictionary to find the meanings.

2. Take some cards. Describe the word on a card without saying it.

3. How many words have… a) 1 syllable, b) 2 syllables, c) 3 syllables, d) 4 syllables, e) 5 syllables, f) 6 syllables?

4. Put words with more than one syllable into groups according to where the strong stress falls.

5. Put the words into alphabetical order.

6. Put together words that have the same number of letters.

7. Put together words that start with the same letter.

8. How many words can you remember when they are all turned over?

Lesson Questions:

1. Where could I go to have my eyes tested and buy some new glasses?

2. a) Put together all the places where I could buy something and think of 5 more kinds of shop. b) What could I buy at each place?

3. Where could I buy some cakes?

4. Put together the places where I could study.

5. Where could I go to pray?

6. Which place is especially for tourists?

7. Which place is still being built?

8. Where could I swim or hire a boat?

9. Where could I go to watch a match?

10. Where could I go to place a bet and either win or lose money?

11. Where could I take my prescription from the doctor's?

12. Where could I borrow books and use a computer?

13. If I wanted to take out some money or pay in a cheque, where would I go?

14. Put these words into order of size: town, city, and village.

Food and Drink

Discussion Words:

milk	carrot	rice	soup
orange	bread	tomato	banana
pizza	mineral water	fruit	cereal
meal	sausage	potato	wine
crisps	cheese	lemonade	lamb
onion	nut	butter	fruit juice
meat	chocolate	fish	flour
vegetable	chicken	apple	egg
pie	chips	food	pasta
strawberry	water	beef	mushroom

Food and Drink

General Questions:

1. Are there any words that you don't know? Use a dictionary to find the meanings.
2. Take some cards. Describe the word on a card without saying it.
3. How many words have... a) 1 syllable, b) 2 syllables, c) 3 syllables, d) 4 syllables?
4. Put words with more than one syllable into groups according to where the strong stress falls.
5. Put the words into alphabetical order.
6. Put together words that have the same number of letters.
7. Put together words that start with the same letter.
8. How many words can you remember when they are all turned over?

Lesson Questions:

1. Which foods do you like? Which foods don't you like? Which foods haven't you tried?
2. Put all the vegetables together in one group and think of 5 more vegetables.
3. Which foods are often served in Italian restaurants?
4. Put all the drinks together in one group and think of 5 more drinks.
5. Which food can be boiled, fried, scrambled, poached, or made into an omelette?
6. Put all the fruits together in one group and think of 5 more fruits.
7. Which food would you eat with fish in a paper parcel?
8. Which foods and drinks are... a) bad for you, b) good for you?
9. Which food can be brown, white, wholemeal, sliced, toasted, and made into rolls?
10. Which drink is white and very good for your teeth and bones?
11. Which word comes after chest-, hazel-, brazil, cashew, wal-, coco-, and pea-?
12. Which drink contains alcohol?
13. a) Put all the different kinds of meat together in one group. b) Put them into your order of preference.
14. Which food can be hard, soft, cream-, cottage-, cheddar, edam, gouda, parmesan, or many more different kinds?

Shopping

Discussion Words:

aisle	local shop	customer	groceries
cash	car park	debit card	price
market	till	sale	way in
promotion	checkout assistant	scales	trolley
change	restaurant	checkout	express lane
queue	manager	supermarket	pence
shelf	bag	cash point	receipt
lift	shopping centre	pounds	way out
bench	refund	delicatessen	money
shop	escalator	opening times	frozen food

Shopping

General Questions:

1. Are there any words that you don't know? Use a dictionary to find the meanings.
2. Take some cards. Describe the word on a card without saying it.
3. How many words have… a) 1 syllable, b) 2 syllables, c) 3 syllables, d) 4 syllables, e) 5 syllables?
4. Put words with more than one syllable into groups according to where the strong stress falls.
5. Put the words into alphabetical order.
6. Put together words that have the same number of letters.
7. Put together words that start with the same letter.
8. How many words can you remember when they are all turned over?

Lesson Questions:

1. Find the word for food and general household shopping.
2. What can I use to buy something? What else could I use?
3. Where can I put my shopping while I'm walking around the supermarket?
4. Who scans my products after I've chosen them?
5. What could I get if I'm not happy with what I've bought?
6. This word means the same as "entrance".
7. Where can I sit down and have a meal?
8. What am I given after I've paid for my shopping?
9. Where can I buy cooked meats, pastries, and cheese?
10. This word means the same as "elevator".
11. This means that some products are being sold at a lower price than usual, or that something has been bought.
12. In the shopping centre or street where can I sit down and have a rest if I feel tired?
13. I can use these to weigh fruit or vegetables before paying for them at the till.
14. I become this if I buy something…

Health

Discussion Words:

infection	bruise	toothbrush	cut
stomach ache	health	emergency	illness
pharmacy	surgery	stethoscope	stretcher
toothpaste	broken bone	hospital	cancer
dentist	injection	stitches	receptionist
headache	waiting room	crutch	ambulance
nurse	fever	tablets	examination
x-ray	doctor	plaster	appointment
prescription	wheelchair	allergy	patient
rash	accident	problem	needle

Complete 12-week Spoken English Course

Health

General Questions:

1. Are there any words that you don't know? Use a dictionary to find the meanings.
2. Take some cards. Describe the word on a card without saying it.
3. How many words have… a) 1 syllable, b) 2 syllables, c) 3 syllables, d) 4 syllables, e) 5 syllables?
4. Put words with more than one syllable into groups according to where the strong stress falls.
5. Put the words into alphabetical order.
6. Put together words that have the same number of letters.
7. Put together words that start with the same letter.
8. How many words can you remember when they are all turned over?

Lesson Questions:

1. Put all the health problems together and put them into order of how serious they are.
2. What could I use to move around if I can't walk?
3. Which word means something urgent?
4. What do I have if someone sticks a needle into me?
5. If I have this I feel hot and sweaty and may see hallucinations.
6. This is done in a hospital so that consultants can see inside of you.
7. How many words end with -ion and what are they?
8. This vehicle is used to take people to and from hospital.
9. Which word sounds like… a) purse, b) wealth, c) news, d) cash, e) lever, f) such?
10. Put together the three words that help keep my teeth healthy.
11. What could I take twice a day if I'm sick?
12. Put all the places together. What can I do in each one?
13. What do I have to make if I want to see my doctor or dentist?
14. A doctor or nurse could use this to listen to my heartbeat.

Sentence Blocks, Discussion Questions, Role Plays, Vocabulary Tests, Verb Forms Practice

Transport

Discussion Words:

fare	petrol pump	tyre	boat
ticket	bus	take-off	motorway
fine	cruise	passenger	canoe
station	driver	train	commuter
engine	aeroplane	ferry	tractor
car	taxi	cancellation	bike
emergency exit	driving licence	car park	road
ship	road sign	reservation	motorbike
flight	service station	airport	roundabout
garage	runway	van	journey

Complete 12-week Spoken English Course

Transport

General Questions:

1. Are there any words that you don't know? Use a dictionary to find the meanings.

2. Take some cards. Describe the word on a card without saying it.

3. How many words have... a) 1 syllable, b) 2 syllables, c) 3 syllables, d) 4 syllables, e) 6 syllables?

4. Put words with more than one syllable into groups according to where the strong stress falls.

5. Put the words into alphabetical order.

6. Put together words that have the same number of letters.

7. Put together words that start with the same letter.

8. How many words can you remember when they are all turned over?

Lesson Questions:

1. I need this if I want to drive a car or motorbike legally.

2. Which words are modes of transport?

3. What do I use to put fuel into my car?

4. This is very annoying when it happens because it means that you will either have to wait, or change your plans altogether.

5. Where can I go to put fuel into my car and buy a snack or some oil?

6. Which modes of transport have you used and which haven't you used?

7. Which word sounds like... a) wrote, b) fuss, c) very, d) fire, e) pair, f) hike?

8. This is what you are if somebody drives you somewhere.

9. Put the modes of transport in order from slowest to fastest.

10. You might have to pay to leave your car here, or it might be free, if you're lucky!

11. Which vehicle is used by farmers in fields?

12. What do I have to pay if I want to travel on a bus, train, or plane?

13. Which modes of transport travel on... a) roads, b) water, c) rails, d) in the sky? Put the words into groups. Can you think of any more modes of transport in each group?

14. This happens when the plane leaves the ground.

Sentence Blocks, Discussion Questions, Role Plays, Vocabulary Tests, Verb Forms Practice

Family

Discussion Words:

boyfriend	mother	son	grandchild
adopted family	father-in-law	girl	niece
granddad	child	grandma	brother-in-law
mother-in-law	foster parent	dad	nephew
mum	uncle	woman	girlfriend
grandson	daughter	parent	brother
baby	ex-	aunt	family
fiancée	sister-in-law	cousin	father
husband	sister	man	partner
boy	fiancé	wife	granddaughter

Family

General Questions:

1. Are there any words that you don't know? Use a dictionary to find the meanings.
2. Take some cards. Describe the word on a card without saying it.
3. How many words have… a) 1 syllable, b) 2 syllables, c) 3 syllables, d) 4 syllables, e) 6 syllables?
4. Put words with more than one syllable into groups according to where the strong stress falls.
5. Put the words into alphabetical order.
6. Put together words that have the same number of letters.
7. Put together words that start with the same letter.
8. How many words can you remember when they are all turned over?

Lesson Questions:

1. Which people are you closest to in your family?
2. Put the words into groups to show which people are… a) female, b) male, c) either.
3. This person is married to my granddad.
4. This person is married to my wife's mother.
5. Which people could be… a) young, b) teenagers/early twenties, c) middle-aged, d) old?
6. This person is my aunt and uncle's child.
7. My dad's sister's husband is his…
8. Which words are not blood relatives?
9. If my son's wife gives birth to a baby girl, I will have a new…
10. Which person is someone that you used to have a relationship with?
11. I'm not engaged to or married to this person, but we're going out with each other.
12. Which words sounds like… a) had, b) aren't, c) maybe, d) mild, e) sun, f) peace?
13. This person looks after me instead of my parents.
14. This is my family, but it's not my original family.

Clothes

Discussion Words:

slipper	zip	vest	tracksuit
tie	buttons	earring	blouse
nightdress	bra	dress	suit
trousers	high heels	t-shirt	jumper
pants	underwear	ring	necklace
tights	jeans	skirt	glasses
shorts	knickers	coat	pyjamas
scarf	sock	belt	shoe
jacket	top	trainer	shirt
handbag	uniform	hat	glove

Clothes

General Questions:

1. Are there any words that you don't know? Use a dictionary to find the meanings.
2. Take some cards. Describe the word on a card without saying it.
3. How many words have… a) 1 syllable, b) 2 syllables, c) 3 syllables?
4. Put words with more than one syllable into groups according to where the strong stress falls.
5. Put the words into alphabetical order.
6. Put together words that have the same number of letters.
7. Put together words that start with the same letter.
8. How many words can you remember when they are all turned over?

Lesson Questions:

1. I need to do these up to keep my jacket or shirt from being open.
2. You may need to wear these to improve your vision.
3. Put together things that only women can wear or use.
4. Which word sounds like… a) sing, b) press, c) you, d) flipper, e) laugh, f) classes?
5. You could wear these if you were going jogging, or exercising at the gym.
6. This is a kind of shirt that women can wear.
7. Which words are kinds of jewellery?
8. Put together all the words to do with underwear.
9. What can be worn under a shirt?
10. You need to wear two of these indoors if you want to keep your feet nice and warm.
11. Put the words into groups according to which clothes are usually cheap and which are usually expensive.
12. What can be worn in bed?
13. Put together things that you would put on to go outside on a cold day.
14. What would you exchange with your new wife or husband when you get married?

Work

Discussion Words:

pharmacist	sales assistant	gardener	plumber
manager	farmer	jeweller	nurse
doctor	mechanic	electrician	florist
artist	admin assistant	painter and decorator	estate agent
accountant	hairdresser	chauffeur	baker
actor	optician	singer	nursery nurse
teacher	newspaper reporter	travel agent	factory worker
receptionist	soldier	builder	lecturer
head teacher	greengrocer	security guard	police officer
train driver	DJ	model	butcher

Work

General Questions:

1. Are there any words that you don't know? Use a dictionary to find the meanings.
2. Take some cards. Describe the word on a card without saying it.
3. How many words have... a) 1 syllable, b) 2 syllables, c) 3 syllables, d) 4 syllables, e) 5 syllables, f) 6 syllables, g) 7 syllables?
4. Put words with more than one syllable into groups according to where the strong stress falls.
5. Put the words into alphabetical order.
6. Put together words that have the same number of letters.
7. Put together words that start with the same letter.
8. How many words can you remember when they are all turned over?

Lesson Questions:

1. Which person could fix some leaky pipes in your bathroom?
2. Which person sells flowers?
3. Put the jobs in order of importance, starting with the most important job.
4. This person plays music at parties or on the radio.
5. This person will help you to either buy or sell a house.
6. Which people can get you from A to B?
7. Put into groups jobs that are... a) well paid, b) have a normal salary, c) low paid?
8. Which person sells watches, rings and necklaces?
9. Put the jobs into order of difficulty, starting with the easiest job.
10. Which person wears clothes (or doesn't wear clothes) for a living?
11. Which person could cut your grass and plant some flowers or shrubs?
12. Which person makes bread and cakes?
13. Which jobs have you done? Which jobs would you... a) like to try, b) never try? Why? / Why not?
14. Which jobs use practical skills and which jobs use intellectual skills?

Home

Discussion Words:

house	carpet	bathroom	light
DVD player	bedroom	apartment	detached house
semi-detached house	bungalow	cooker	flat
cupboard	garden	dining room	washing machine
fireplace	kitchen	door	garage
freezer	ceiling	stairs	wall
fridge	radiator	television	sideboard
hall	floor	toilet	sink
living room	dining chair	bed	bath
shower	sofa	dining table	wardrobe

Complete 12-week Spoken English Course

Home

General Questions:

1. Are there any words that you don't know? Use a dictionary to find the meanings.
2. Take some cards. Describe the word on a card without saying it.
3. How many words have… a) 1 syllable, b) 2 syllables, c) 3 syllables, d) 4 syllables, e) 5 syllables?
4. Put words with more than one syllable into groups according to where the strong stress falls.
5. Put the words into alphabetical order.
6. Put together words that have the same number of letters.
7. Put together words that start with the same letter.
8. How many words can you remember when they are all turned over?

Lesson Questions:

1. What do you use to get to the next floor in a house?
2. This is the first room that you come into when you enter a house.
3. Which word sounds like… a) poor, b) think, c) fall, d) mouse, e) right, f) bridge?
4. Which words are kinds of accommodation? Put them in order of price.
5. This is where I store dry foods such as pasta, rice, tins of beans, and biscuits.
6. We normally eat our main meals together in this room.
7. Which room is home to the cooker, fridge and sideboard?
8. We have these in most rooms and switch them on when we want to keep warm.
9. This covers the floor in some of the rooms in my house.
10. This is where you could go outside to relax and read a book – or do some planting.
11. If I stand in any room in my house and look up what will I see?
12. It's great to lie in a hot one of these to unwind after a long and busy day.
13. Which things would you find in the… a) living room, b) bathroom, c) kitchen, d) dining room, e) bedroom?
14. Without these the ceiling would be on the floor!

Sentence Blocks, Discussion Questions, Role Plays, Vocabulary Tests, Verb Forms Practice

Free Time

Discussion Words:

tent	swimming pool	internet	tennis
fishing	cooking	camping	relaxation
hobby	cinema	hiking	picnic
volleyball	hotel	computer game	cycling
leisure centre	sleeping bag	rugby	park
skiing	holiday	theatre	climbing
swimming	reading	watching TV	weekend
sport	football	café	safari park
bowling club	playground	jogging	sunbathing
golf	basketball	beach	amusement park

Complete 12-week Spoken English Course

Free Time

General Questions:

1. Are there any words that you don't know? Use a dictionary to find the meanings.
2. Take some cards. Describe the word on a card without saying it.
3. How many words have… a) 1 syllable, b) 2 syllables, c) 3 syllables, d) 4 syllables?
4. Put words with more than one syllable into groups according to where the strong stress falls.
5. Put the words into alphabetical order.
6. Put together words that have the same number of letters.
7. Put together words that start with the same letter.
8. How many words can you remember when they are all turned over?

Lesson Questions:

1. This is a place where you go to see wild animals up close, such as bears and tigers.
2. Which word sounds like… a) dark, b) bought, c) looking, d) motel, e) reach, f) went?
3. Which words are connected with physical exercise?
4. Which words are places that you could go to?
5. For this activity you could use a magazine, newspaper, book, or laptop.
6. Which activity involves living in the open air close to nature?
7. This is the great feeling you get when you take a break from work and start to unwind.
8. Which words are to do with… a) indoor activities, and b) outdoor activities?
9. Which word means Saturday and Sunday together?
10. Which word could be played on a PC, Mac, Xbox 360, Nintendo Wii, or Playstation?
11. These are places where you could watch… a) a film, b) a play.
12. This is where you can join a gym, do aerobics, have a sauna or massage, and swim.
13. This is a generally passive activity and doesn't encourage a lot of movement or require much thought. You simply have to sit and stare at the box…
14. a) Put all the sports together. b) Put them into order, from your favourite to your least favourite sports.

Complete 12-week Spoken English Course

_____ / **Town**

Vocabulary Test:

First Language:	English:
_____	bank
_____	post office
_____	church
_____	clothes shop
_____	library
_____	river
_____	optician's
_____	bridge
_____	public toilets
_____	department store
_____	market place
_____	bus stop
_____	apartment block
_____	lake
_____	city
_____	traffic lights
_____	tennis court
_____	office
_____	bakery
_____	village

Complete 12-week Spoken English Course

_____ / **Food and Drink**

Vocabulary Test:

First Language:	*English:*
_____	meal
_____	fruit
_____	lemonade
_____	fish
_____	fruit juice
_____	cereal
_____	cheese
_____	chips
_____	meat
_____	pasta
_____	food
_____	potato
_____	bread
_____	soup
_____	rice
_____	chocolate
_____	vegetable
_____	water
_____	egg
_____	wine

Sentence Blocks, Discussion Questions, Role Plays, Vocabulary Tests, Verb Forms Practice

Complete 12-week Spoken English Course

_____ / **Shopping**

Vocabulary Test:

First Language:	*English:*
_____	car park
_____	sale
_____	restaurant
_____	supermarket
_____	trolley
_____	way in
_____	groceries
_____	cash
_____	checkout assistant
_____	debit card
_____	receipt
_____	refund
_____	lift
_____	price
_____	queue
_____	shopping centre
_____	frozen food
_____	shop
_____	way out
_____	delicatessen

Complete 12-week Spoken English Course

_____ / **Health**

Vocabulary Test:

First Language: *English:*

_____   health

_____   waiting room

_____   appointment

_____   receptionist

_____   tablets

_____   prescription

_____   problem

_____   examination

_____   doctor

_____   nurse

_____   dentist

_____   hospital

_____   surgery

_____   pharmacy

_____   emergency

_____   ambulance

_____   illness

_____   allergy

_____   accident

_____   injection

_____ / Transport

Vocabulary Test:

First Language:	English:
_____	bus
_____	train
_____	taxi
_____	station
_____	bike
_____	motorway
_____	ticket
_____	reservation
_____	aeroplane
_____	flight
_____	journey
_____	cancellation
_____	commuter
_____	passenger
_____	driver
_____	car
_____	motorbike
_____	airport
_____	garage
_____	driving licence

Complete 12-week Spoken English Course

_____ / **Family**

Vocabulary Test:

First Language: *English:*

_____ dad

_____ aunt

_____ nephew

_____ husband

_____ cousin

_____ uncle

_____ grandma

_____ mum

_____ sister

_____ daughter

_____ granddad

_____ ex-

_____ niece

_____ son

_____ granddaughter

_____ partner

_____ brother

_____ grandson

_____ parent

_____ wife

Complete 12-week Spoken English Course

_____ / **Clothes**

<u>Vocabulary Test:</u>

First Language:	_English:_
_____	trousers
_____	skirt
_____	blouse
_____	sock
_____	shoe
_____	jumper
_____	jacket
_____	hat
_____	coat
_____	underwear
_____	dress
_____	tie
_____	scarf
_____	glasses
_____	suit
_____	shirt
_____	top
_____	pyjamas
_____	uniform
_____	jeans

Complete 12-week Spoken English Course

_____ / **Work**

Vocabulary Test:

First Language: *English:*

_____   plumber

_____   manager

_____   nurse

_____   electrician

_____   doctor

_____   mechanic

_____   admin assistant

_____   accountant

_____   hairdresser

_____   singer

_____   nursery nurse

_____   teacher

_____   factory worker

_____   builder

_____   police officer

_____   train driver

_____   optician

_____   actor

_____   farmer

_____   model

Sentence Blocks, Discussion Questions, Role Plays, Vocabulary Tests, Verb Forms Practice

Complete 12-week Spoken English Course

_____ / **Home**

Vocabulary Test:

First Language:	English:
_____	house
_____	bedroom
_____	garden
_____	stairs
_____	fridge
_____	washing machine
_____	apartment
_____	bed
_____	television
_____	bath
_____	living room
_____	sofa
_____	toilet
_____	wardrobe
_____	sink
_____	cooker
_____	kitchen
_____	cupboard
_____	bathroom
_____	dining room

Sentence Blocks, Discussion Questions, Role Plays, Vocabulary Tests, Verb Forms Practice

Complete 12-week Spoken English Course

_____ / **Free Time**

Vocabulary Test:

First Language:	*English:*
_____	cinema
_____	theatre
_____	bowling club
_____	café
_____	park
_____	leisure centre
_____	swimming pool
_____	tennis
_____	football
_____	amusement park
_____	golf
_____	swimming
_____	rugby
_____	volleyball
_____	camping
_____	cycling
_____	holiday
_____	weekend
_____	reading
_____	computer game

Lesson Test – Town

A) *Put a mark above the stressed syllable in each word or phrase and write how many syllables there are:*

a) post office ( )   b) library ( )   c) bakery ( )   d) office ( )   e) public toilets ( )

B) *Complete the gap in each starting sentence with one of these words:*

　　　　a) ran　　　b) cycling　　　c) drive　　　d) walks

1. Peter _____ two kilometres to his office every day.

2. Jennifer bought a couple of cakes at the bakery, then _____ to the post office.

3. We could _____ to the lake and go fishing.

C) *Underline the word that is different in each group and state why:*

1. a) department store   b) town hall   c) bakery   d) butcher's   _____
2. a) casino   b) tennis court   c) park   d) football stadium   _____
3. a) bus stop   b) traffic lights   c) school   d) pavement   _____
4. a) church   b) office   c) cathedral   d) mosque   _____

Complete the sentence blocks:

D) Verb Form: _____

- I've agreed to meet Dan in the old market place outside the library.
- Who   1. _____ you agreed to meet in the old market place outside the library?
- 2. _____.
- Have you agreed   3. _____ Dan in the old market place outside the library?
- Yes, I   4. _____.
- Have you agreed to meet   5. _____ in the old market place outside the library?
- No,   6. _____. I haven't agreed to meet Alex in the old market place outside the library.

E) Verb Form: _____

- The new optician's next to the bank will open next Friday.
- 7. _____ will the new optician's next to the bank open?
- Next   8. _____.
- 9. _____ the new optician's next to the bank open next Friday?
- Yes,   10. _____ will.
- Will the new optician's next to the bank open next   11. _____?
- No, it   12. _____. The new optician's next to the bank won't open next Saturday.

Complete 12-week Spoken English Course

Lesson Test – Food and Drink

A) *Translate these words into English from the International Phonetic Alphabet (IPA):*

a) /mɪlk/ _____   d) /fruːt/ _____
b) /bred/ _____   e) /'tʃɒklət/ _____
c) /tʃiːz/ _____   f) /waɪn/ _____

B) *Fill in the missing words in these sentence block starting sentences:*

1. Michelle is having salad and pasta because she doesn't _____ meat.

2. Potatoes _____ be boiled, mashed, fried, chipped, roasted or oven-baked.

3. Daniel gave _____ the largest portion of ice cream.

4. We're _____ to buy some fruit at the supermarket this afternoon.

5. Jenny has _____ put the cheese in the fridge.

C) *Write a food or drink word that sounds like:*

1. please   2. red   3. feet   4. hips   5. leg   6. nice   7. but

_____

Complete the sentence blocks:

D) Verb Form: _____

- The best kind of bread is white sliced bread.
- What   1. _____ the best kind of bread?
- White sliced   2. _____.
- 3. _____ white sliced bread the best kind of bread?
- Yes,   4. _____ is.
- Is dry wholemeal bread the   5. _____ kind of bread?
- No, it   6. _____. Dry wholemeal bread isn't the best kind of bread.

E) Verb Form: _____

- If you eat too much chocolate you will put on weight.
- 7. _____ will happen if I eat too much chocolate?
- You will   8. _____.
- 9. _____ I put on weight if I eat too much chocolate?
- Yes, you   10. _____.
- Will I   11. _____ if I eat too much chocolate?
- 12. _____, you won't. You won't lose weight if you eat too much chocolate.

Sentence Blocks, Discussion Questions, Role Plays, Vocabulary Tests, Verb Forms Practice

Lesson Test – Shopping

A) *Match together the two halves of each word; then write the words:*

1. ceries
2. lator
3. ger
4. ckout
5. rket
6. ion

a) mana
b) superma
c) promot
d) esca
e) gro
f) che

_____
_____
_____
_____
_____
_____

B) *Sentence stress: underline the content words in each starting sentence:*

1. I've looked everywhere in this shop for a tin of vegetable soup, but I can't find one anywhere.
2. Jan was leaving the car park because she had finished her shopping.
3. We should take the lift to the fifth floor.
4. Simon is visiting the new shopping centre near St. Mark's Road.

C) *Unscramble the shopping words:*

1. ericp   2. cenep   3. ceirtep   4. gab   5. sundop   6. itll   7. elas

_____

Complete the sentence blocks:

D) Verb Form: _____

- Emma is the manager of a small Italian restaurant.
- 1. _____ is the manager of a small Italian restaurant?
- Emma 2. _____.
- Is Emma the manager of 3._____?
- Yes, 4. _____ is.
- 5. _____ Bill the manager of a small Italian restaurant?
- 6. _____, he isn't. Bill isn't the manager of a small Italian restaurant.

E) Verb Form: _____

- I used my debit card to buy a pair of shoes for work.
- What did you 7. _____ to buy a pair of shoes for work?
- 8. _____ debit card.
- 9. _____ your debit card to buy a pair of shoes for work?
- Yes, I 10. _____.
- Did you use cash 11. _____ buy a pair of shoes for work?
- No, I 12. _____. I didn't use cash to buy a pair of shoes for work.

Lesson Test – Health

A) *Fill in the missing vowels in these health words:*

1. h ___ ___ d ___ ch ___
2. ___ cc ___ d ___ nt
3. ___ lln ___ ss
4. ___ nf ___ ct ___ ___ n
5. ___ m ___ rg ___ ncy
6. ___ mb ___ l ___ nc ___

B) *Complete the verbs in each starting sentence:*

1. Sammi i_____ s_____ in the waiting room with her mum and brother.
2. Being healthy i_____ very important to me.
3. Simon i_____ g_____ to v_____ the optician's for an eye examination.
4. I p_____ my doctor this morning to m_____ an appointment.

C) *Underline the odd one out in each group of health words and give a reason:*

1. receptionist, dentist, nurse, appointment
2. surgery, hospital, allergy, waiting room
3. plaster, broken bone, fever, stomach ache
4. patient, health, pharmacy, prescription

Complete the sentence blocks:

D) Verb Form: _____

- Kenny has to take his prescription to the pharmacy tomorrow.
- When 1. _____ Kenny have to take his prescription to the pharmacy?
- 2. _____.
- 3. _____ Kenny have to take his prescription to the pharmacy tomorrow?
- Yes, he 4. _____.
- Does Kenny 5. _____ his prescription to the pharmacy next Monday?
- No, he 6. _____. Kenny doesn't have to take his prescription to the pharmacy next Monday.

E) Verb Form: _____

- Ella was telling the receptionist about her husband's painful arthritis.
- Who 7. _____ telling the receptionist about her husband's painful arthritis?
- 8. _____ was.
- Was Ella 9. _____ the receptionist about her husband's painful arthritis?
- Yes, 10. _____ was.
- 11. _____ Joanne telling the receptionist about her husband's painful arthritis?
- 12. _____, she wasn't. Joanne wasn't telling the receptionist about her husband's painful arthritis.

Lesson Test – Transport

A) *Write these starting sentences in the correct order:*

1. our   because   we've   flight   daughter   our   ill   cancelled   is
_____

2. he   when   was   bus   Oliver   by   hit   road   a   crossing   the   was
_____

B) *Complete the verbs in each starting sentence:*

1. Gemma i_____ d_____ to the airport to pick up her grandmother.
2. The next train to a_____ at platform 8 w_____ be the 9.49 service to Cardiff.
3. If we c_____ to work we'll g_____ there in about an hour.
4. All passengers must s_____ their passports and boarding passes at the gate.

C) *Sentence stress: mark the correct stress pattern for this starting sentence:* "I flew from Heathrow to Copenhagen last night".

        a) ● ● ● ● ● ●

        b) ● ● ● ● ● ●

Complete the sentence blocks:

D) Verb Form: _____

- I flew from Heathrow to Copenhagen last night.
- What did you   1. _____ last night?
- I   2. _____ from Heathrow to Copenhagen.
- 3. _____ you fly from Heathrow to Copenhagen last night?
- Yes, I   4. _____.
- Did you   5. _____ the cinema last night?
- 6. _____, I didn't. I didn't go to the cinema last night.

E) Verb Form: _____

- I usually get the train at 7.28.
- 7. _____ do you usually get the train?
- 8. _____ 7.28.
- Do   9. _____ usually get the train at 7.28?
- Yes,   10. _____ do.
- 11. _____ you usually get the train at 7.48?
- No, I   12. _____. I don't usually get the train at 7.48.

Complete 12-week Spoken English Course

Lesson Test – Family

A) *Complete the sentences:*

1. My mother's brother is my _____.
2. My grandmother's granddaughter is my _____, or my _____.
3. My sister's son is my _____.
4. My uncle's sister is my _____, or my _____.

B) *Which starting sentences from this unit are wrong? Make corrections below:*

1. My grandparents have decided to go on holiday to Florida next year.
2. If our parents get divorced the family will be very disappointed.
3. My sister was walking to the library with her children when she saw a wasp.
4. Jenna's aunt and uncle visited us in June because they wanted to see our new baby.

C) *Write 8 family words in alphabetical order; do not include words from question A):*

_____
_____

Complete the sentence blocks:

D) Verb Form: _____

- Your grandma and granddad should think about moving into a retirement bungalow.
- 1. _____ grandma and granddad should think about moving into a retirement bungalow?
- 2. _____ grandma and granddad should.
- Should 3. _____ grandma and granddad think about moving into a retirement bungalow?
- Yes, 4. _____ should.
- 5. _____ my friend's grandma and granddad think about moving into a retirement bungalow?
- No, they 6. _____. Your friend's grandma and granddad shouldn't think about moving into a retirement bungalow.

E) Verb Form: _____

- Roberto's daughter is playing with her cousins.
- What 7. _____ Roberto's daughter doing?
- 8. _____ with her cousins.
- 9. _____ Roberto's daughter playing with her cousins?
- Yes, she 10. _____.
- Is 11. _____ watching TV with her cousins?
- 12. _____, she isn't. Roberto's daughter isn't watching TV with her cousins.

Sentence Blocks, Discussion Questions, Role Plays, Vocabulary Tests, Verb Forms Practice

Complete 12-week Spoken English Course

Lesson Test – Clothes

A) *Find the clothes in these mixed-up words:*

1) resds   2) usroesrt   3) finmuor   4) kajtec   5) sgesals   6) ite   7) uleobs

_____

B) *Match the halves of these starting sentences:*

1. I wear glasses
2. We'll have a clearout of our wardrobe
3. Stephen has to wear
4. If you wear a suit and tie to the interview

a) a blue and grey uniform every day for his job as a security guard.
b) because I'm short-sighted.
c) you'll make an excellent impression.
d) to see what we can give away to charity.

C) *Read the starting sentences and cross out the unnecessary word in each one:*

1. Harry is been trying on a new pair of smart black trousers.
2. Frankie bought herself a new dress but and some underwear in the trendiest boutique on Oxford Street.

Complete the sentence blocks:

D) Verb Form: _____

- Michael was wearing the yellow and brown striped pyjamas that his grandma had knitted him for Christmas.
- Who 1. _____ the yellow and brown striped pyjamas that his grandma had knitted him for Christmas?
- Michael 2. _____.
- Was Michael 3. _____ the yellow and brown striped pyjamas that his grandma had knitted him for Christmas?
- Yes, 4. _____.
- 5. _____ Paul wearing the yellow and brown striped pyjamas that his grandma had knitted him for Christmas?
- No, he wasn't. Paul 6. _____ the yellow and brown striped pyjamas that his grandma had knitted him for Christmas.

E) Verb Form: _____

- I have always liked jackets and tops from Marks and Spencer.
- What 7. _____?
- Jackets and 8. _____.
- 9. _____ you always liked jackets and tops from Marks and Spencer?
- Yes, I 10. _____.
- Have you 11. _____ liked jackets and tops from ASDA?
- No, I haven't. 12. _____ liked jackets and tops from ASDA.

94

Sentence Blocks, Discussion Questions, Role Plays, Vocabulary Tests, Verb Forms Practice

Lesson Test – Work

A) *Sentence stress: write the content words from two starting sentences in the correct order (1, 2, 3, etc.):*

    i)   working   business   Gerry   dad's   furniture   hates   part-time

    ii)   been   Jo   August   friend   unemployed   last

B) *Write the correct spelling for each of these jobs:*

1. jeweler   2. chuffeur   3. estate agant   4. bilder   5. nerse   6. teecher

7. factry worker   8. acter   9. hairdreser   10. train driwer   11. acountant   12. JD

C) *Read the starting sentences and cross out the unnecessary word in each one:*

1. Edward was updating his CV because Edward he wanted to apply for a new job.
2. When Greg was worked for Dell he had to do plenty of overtime.
3. Dave will have to work very hard if he is wants to have a successful career in sales.
4. I'm going to visit that new employment agency about the temporary work.

Complete the sentence blocks:

D) Verb Form: _____

- Helena is hoping to get promoted at the end of the year.
- When is Helena 1. _____?
- 2. _____ of the year.
- 3. _____ Helena hoping to get promoted at the end of the year?
- 4. _____, she is.
- Is Helena 5. _____ promoted next March?
- No, 6. _____. Helena isn't hoping to get promoted next March.

E) Verb Form: _____

- You need to ask your manager for a pay rise as soon as possible!
- 7. _____ do I need to ask my manager for as soon as possible?
- For a 8. _____.
- 9. _____ I need to ask my manager for a pay rise as soon as possible?
- Yes, you 10. _____.
- Do 11. _____ need to ask my manager for more work as soon as possible?
- No, you 12. _____. You don't need to ask your manager for more work as soon as possible.

Lesson Test – Home

A) *Write these words in alphabetical order:*

fridge   cooker   door   carpet   bathroom   ceiling   bungalow   freezer   cupboard   fireplace   bath

_____

B) *Write a home word that sounds like:*

  1. more   2. pears   3. night   4. mouse   5. power   6. ball

_____

C) *Underline the wrongly spelled word in each starting sentence and write each word correctly:*

1. When I went to their home Jack and Lisa showd me their new bathroom.
2. Mark is buying a new washing machin because his old one is broken.
3. If you sell your horrible flat youl be able to put down a deposit on a nice house.
4. I'll do the hoovering quickly befor I have a bath.
5. Sarah and Noel were wtching funny DVDs in their living room for three hours last night.
6. Barry has to do the washing up every nite after tea.

Complete the sentence blocks:

D) Verb Form: _____

- Jason has finished cutting the grass in the back garden.
- 1. _____ has Jason finished doing in the back garden?
- 2. _____.
- 3. _____ Jason finished cutting the grass in the back garden?
- Yes, he   4. _____.
- Has   5. _____ watering the plants in the back garden?
- No, he   6. _____. Jason hasn't finished watering the plants in the back garden.

E) Verb Form: _____

- I live in a small semi-detached house in Manchester.
- Where   7. _____ live?
- 8. _____ a small semi-detached house in Manchester.
- Do   9. _____ live in a small semi-detached house in Manchester?
- Yes,   10. _____.
- 11. _____ you live in a large detached house in Wimbledon?
- No, I don't. I   12. _____ in a large detached house in Wimbledon.

Complete 12-week Spoken English Course

Lesson Test – Free Time

A) *Write the correct spelling for these words to do with free time:*

1. campin	2. teatre	3. piknic	4. climing	5. parc	6. swiming pool
7. beatch	8. hottel	9. reeding	10. caffé	11. couking	12. sleping bag

B) *Match the halves of these starting sentences:*

1. Chester's son was playing golf badly yesterday afternoon
2. I have seen Macbeth
3. Me, Jess and Casey
4. I love going to the cinema with my friends,

a) at this theatre five times.
b) because we always have a good time.
c) with a few friends from his cousin's bowling club.
d) are going to watch the tennis in the park.

C) *Write the names of 10 different sports or leisure activities in alphabetical order:*
_____
_____

Complete the Sentence Blocks:

D) Verb Form: _____

- We went on a camping holiday last summer for two weeks, but I was bored because it rained every day.
- How long 1. _____ you go on a camping holiday for last summer?
- For 2. _____.
- Did you go 3. _____ a camping holiday last summer for two weeks?
- Yes, 4. _____ did.
- 5. _____ you go on a camping holiday last summer for a week?
- 6. _____, we didn't. We didn't go on a camping holiday last summer for a week.

E) Verb Form: _____

- Barney and Wanda are enjoying a day out at an amusement park.
- Who 7. _____ enjoying a day out at an amusement park?
- 8. _____.
- 9. _____ Barney and Wanda enjoying a day out at an amusement park?
- Yes, they 10. _____.
- Are 11. _____ enjoying a day out at an amusement park?
- No, 12. _____. Alex and Sue aren't enjoying a day out at an amusement park.

Sentence Blocks, Discussion Questions, Role Plays, Vocabulary Tests, Verb Forms Practice

Present Simple

Sentence Blocks:

1. Peter walks two kilometres to his office every day.
Who

2. The best kind of bread is white sliced bread.
What

3. Emma is the manager of a small Italian restaurant.
Who

4. Being healthy is very important to me.
What

5. I usually get the train at 7.28.
When

6. My mum lives with her new partner in Brighton.
Where

7. I wear glasses because I'm short-sighted.
Why

8. Gerry hates working part-time for his dad's furniture business.
Who

9. I live in a small semi-detached house in Manchester.
Where

10. I love going to the cinema with my friends, because we always have a good time.
Why

Present Continuous

<u>Sentence Blocks:</u>

1. We're waiting patiently for the bus at the bus stop opposite the church.
Where

2. Michelle is having salad and pasta because she doesn't eat meat.
Why

3. Simon is visiting the new shopping centre near St. Mark's Road.
What

4. Sammy is sitting in the waiting room with her mum and brother.
Where

5. Gemma is driving to the airport to pick up her grandmother.
Where

6. Roberto's daughter is playing with her cousins.
What

7. Harry is trying on a new pair of smart black trousers.
Who

8. Helena is hoping to get promoted at the end of the year.
When

9. Mark is buying a new washing machine because his old one is broken.
Why

10. Barney and Wanda are enjoying a day out at an amusement park.
Who

Past Simple

Sentence Blocks:

1. Jennifer bought a couple of cakes at the bakery, then ran to the post office.
What

2. Daniel gave himself the largest portion of ice cream.
Who

3. I used my debit card to buy a pair of shoes for work.
What

4. I phoned my doctor this morning to make an appointment.
Why

5. I flew from Heathrow to Copenhagen last night.
What

6. Jenna's aunt and uncle visited us in May because they wanted to see our new baby.
Why

7. Frankie bought herself a new dress and some underwear in the trendiest boutique on Oxford Street.
Where

8. When Greg worked for Dell he had to do plenty of overtime.
What

9. When I went to their home Jack and Lisa showed me their new bathroom.
What

10. We went on a camping holiday last summer for two weeks.
How long

Past Continuous

Sentence Blocks:

1. The department store was opening until 10 o'clock because they were having a massive sale.
Why

2. Ellen was talking about her sister who loves fish and chips.
Who

3. Jan was leaving the car park because she had finished her shopping.
Why

4. Ella was telling the receptionist about her husband's painful arthritis.
Who

5. Oliver was crossing the road when he was hit by a bus.
Who

6. My sister was walking to the city museum with her children when she saw a fox.
Where

7. Michael was wearing the yellow and brown striped pyjamas that his grandma had knitted him for Christmas.
Who

8. Edward was updating his CV because he wanted to apply for a new job.
Why

9. Sarah and Noel were watching funny DVDs in their living room for three hours last night. *Who*

10. Chester's son was playing golf badly yesterday afternoon with a few friends from his cousin's bowling club. *How*

Present Perfect

<u>Sentence Blocks:</u>

1. I've agreed to meet Dan in the old market place outside the library.
Who

2. Jenny has just put the cheese in the fridge.
Where

3. I've looked everywhere in this shop for a tin of vegetable soup, but I can't find one anywhere.
Where

4. I've taken two tablets three times a day for a week, but I don't feel any better.
How many

5. We've cancelled our flight because our daughter is ill.
Why

6. The whole family has decided to go on holiday to Florida next year.
Who

7. I have always liked jackets and tops from Marks and Spencer.
What

8. My friend Jo has been unemployed since last August.
How long

9. Jason has finished cutting the grass in the back garden.
What

10. I have seen Macbeth at this theatre five times.
How many

Modal Verbs

Sentence Blocks:

1. We could drive to the lake and go fishing.
Where

2. Potatoes can be boiled, mashed, fried, chipped, roasted or oven-baked.
How

3. We should take the lift to the fifth floor.
What

4. Kenny has to take his prescription to the pharmacy tomorrow.
When

5. All passengers must show their passports and boarding passes at the gate.
What

6. Your grandma and granddad should think about moving into a retirement bungalow.
Whose

7. Stephen has to wear a blue and grey uniform every day for his job as a security guard.
When

8. You need to ask your manager for a pay rise as soon as possible!
What

9. Barry has to do the washing up every night after tea.
How often

10. You should do some exercise instead of playing computer games all day. *What*

Future Forms

<u>Sentence Blocks:</u>

1. The new optician's next to the bank will open next Friday.
When

2. We're going to buy some fruit at the supermarket this afternoon.
What

3. After we finish buying groceries, we'll go to Nero's for a quick coffee.
When

4. Simon is going to visit the optician's for an eye examination.
Why

5. The next train to arrive at platform 8 will be the 9.49 service to Cardiff.
Which

6. Sam's brother is going to start university in Edinburgh next September.
When

7. We'll have a clearout of our wardrobe to see what we can give away to charity.
Why

8. I'm going to visit that new employment agency about temporary work.
Where

9. I'll do the hoovering quickly before I have a bath.
When

10. Me, Jess and Casey are going to watch the tennis in the park.
Where

Complete 12-week Spoken English Course

First Conditional

Sentence Blocks:

1. If the tennis court is busy we can go to the gym instead.
What

2. If you eat too much chocolate you will put on weight.
What

3. If the checkout assistant offers to pack my bags I'll let her.
What

4. If you ask the doctor she will give you some good advice about your problem.
What

5. If we cycle to work we'll get there in about an hour.
When

6. If our parents get divorced the family will be very disappointed.
What

7. If you wear a suit and tie to the interview you'll make an excellent impression.
What kind

8. Dave will have to work very hard if he wants to have a successful career in sales.
What

9. If you sell your horrible flat you'll be able to put down a deposit on a nice house.
What

10. If the leisure centre is still open we can all go swimming.   *What*

Complete 12-week Spoken English Course

End of Course Oral Examination (Page 1)

Name: _____ Date: _____ Total # Marks: _____ /100

Question 1
Form the sentence block:

Peter walks two kilometres to his office every day.

Who walks two kilometres to his office every day?

Peter does.

Does Peter walk two kilometres to his office every day?

Yes, he does.

Does Jeff walk two kilometres to his office every day?
(Answers will vary)

No, he doesn't. Jeff doesn't walk two kilometres to his office every day.
(Answers will vary)

Which verb form is used in the starting sentence? (Answer: present simple) (8 marks)

Question 2
Tell me ten different members of a family, e.g. mother.

See page 68 for a list of family words. (10 marks)

Question 3
Describe your dream home. Where would you like to live if you could live anywhere? Talk about location, type of home, number of rooms, furniture, swimming pool, garden, staff, etc.

(4 marks)

Question 4
Put these clothes words into alphabetical order: trainers, coat, scarf, dress, belt, sock.

Answer: belt, coat, dress, scarf, sock, trainers.

(1 mark)

Complete 12-week Spoken English Course

End of Course Oral Examination (Page 2)

Question 5
Form the sentence block:

If you ask the doctor she will give you some good advice about your problem. ☐

Who will give me some good advice about my problem if I ask her? ☐

The doctor will. ☐

Will the doctor give me some good advice about my problem if I ask her? ☐

Yes, she will. ☐

Will the receptionist give me some good advice about my problem if I ask her? ☐
(Answers will vary)

No, they won't. The receptionist won't give you some good advice about your problem if you ask them. ☐
(Answers will vary)

Which verb form is used in the starting sentence? (Answer: first conditional) ☐ (8 marks)

Question 6
What is your favourite food? Why do you like it? How often do you eat it? What is your favourite drink? Why?

(4 marks) ☐

Question 7
Tell me ten different jobs, e.g. doctor.

See page 64 for a list of health words. (10 marks) ☐

Question 8
Tell me two forms of transport that have:

a) 1 syllable ☐   c) 3 syllables ☐

b) 2 syllables ☐

Answers will vary. See page 66 for a list of transport words. Suggested answers: a) bus, train; b) canoe, ferry; c) motorbike, aeroplane. (6 marks)

Sentence Blocks, Discussion Questions, Role Plays, Vocabulary Tests, Verb Forms Practice

Complete 12-week Spoken English Course

End of Course Oral Examination (Page 3)

Question 9
Form the sentence block:

After we finish buying groceries, we'll go to Nero's for a quick coffee.

Where will we go for a quick coffee after we finish buying groceries?

To Nero's.

Will we go to Nero's for a quick coffee after we finish buying groceries?

Yes, we will.

Will we go to Bob's Coffee Shop for a quick coffee after we finish buying groceries?
(Answers will vary)

No, we won't. We won't go to Bob's Coffee Shop for a quick coffee after we finish buying groceries
(Answers will vary)

Which verb form is used in the starting sentence? (Answer: future forms) (8 marks)

Question 10
Which family word has a different word stress from the others? Why?

family, fiancé, granddaughter

Answer: The word *fiancé* has a different word stress because the strong stress falls on the second syllable, while in *family* and *granddaughter* the strong stress falls on the first syllable.

(1 mark)

Question 11
Tell me about a memorable holiday. Where was it? Who did you go with? Why did you decide to go there? What happened?

(4 marks)

Question 12
Tell me ten different modes of transport, e.g. bicycle.

See page 66 for a list of transport words.   (10 marks)

Sentence Blocks, Discussion Questions, Role Plays, Vocabulary Tests, Verb Forms Practice

Complete 12-week Spoken English Course

End of Course Oral Examination (Page 4)

Question 13
Form the sentence block:

I have seen Macbeth at this theatre five times.

How many times have you seen Macbeth at this theatre?

Five times.

Have you seen Macbeth at this theatre five times?

Yes, I have.

Have you seen Macbeth at this theatre six times?
(Answers will vary)

No, I haven't. I haven't seen Macbeth at this theatre six times.
(Answers will vary)

Which verb form is used in the starting sentence? (Answer: present perfect) (8 marks)

Question 14
If you were given £3,000 to spend only on clothes and shoes, what would you buy and where would you go shopping?

(4 marks)

Question 15
Tell me ten different kinds of food, e.g. pasta.

See page 60 for a list of food words.   (10 marks)

Question 16
Which person...

a) can fix a leaky pipe?   c) sells flowers?

b) can help you sell your house?   d) wears clothes for a living?

Answers: a) plumber, b) estate agent, c) florist, d) model   (4 marks)

Sentence Blocks, Discussion Questions, Role Plays, Vocabulary Tests, Verb Forms Practice

Complete 12-week Spoken English Course

Elementary Level

Certificate in Spoken English

This is to certify that:

_____

has completed a _____ week Talk a Lot course in spoken English at this establishment and has achieved the following grade:

Grade: _____

Achievement: _____

Date: _____

Candidate Number: _____

Signed: _____ (Course Teacher) Date: _____

Signed: _____ (Centre Manager) Date: _____

School Name and Address:

School Phone Number / Email Address / Website Address:

Sentence Blocks, Discussion Questions, Role Plays, Vocabulary Tests, Verb Forms Practice

Complete 12-week Spoken English Course

Elementary Level

Certificate in Spoken English

This is to certify that:

_____

has completed a _____ week Talk a Lot course in spoken English at this establishment and has achieved the following grade:

Grade: _____

Achievement: _____

Subjects Covered:

- ✓ Speaking and Listening
- ✓ Pronunciation
- ✓ Grammar
- ✓ Vocabulary
- ✓ Word and Sentence Stress

Date: _____

Candidate Number: _____

Signed: _____ (Course Teacher) Date: _____

Signed: _____ (Centre Manager) Date: _____

School Name and Address:

School Phone Number / Email Address / Website Address:

Sentence Blocks, Discussion Questions, Role Plays, Vocabulary Tests, Verb Forms Practice

Complete 12-week Spoken English Course

Elementary Level

Certificate in Spoken English

This is to certify that:

_____

has completed a _____ week Talk a Lot course in spoken English at this establishment and has achieved the following grade:

Grade: _____

Achievement: _____

Date: _____

Candidate Number: _____

Signed: _____ (Course Teacher) Date: _____

Signed: _____ (Centre Manager) Date: _____

School Name and Address:

School Phone Number / Email Address / Website Address:

Sentence Blocks, Discussion Questions, Role Plays, Vocabulary Tests, Verb Forms Practice

Complete 12-week Spoken English Course

Elementary Level

Certificate in Spoken English

This is to certify that:

_____

has completed a _____ week Talk a Lot course in spoken English at this establishment and has achieved the following grade:

Grade: _____

Achievement: _____

Subjects Covered:

- ✓ Speaking and Listening
- ✓ Pronunciation
- ✓ Grammar
- ✓ Vocabulary
- ✓ Word and Sentence Stress

Date: _____

Candidate Number: _____

Signed: _____ (Course Teacher)   Date: _____

Signed: _____ (Centre Manager)   Date: _____

School Name and Address:

School Phone Number / Email Address / Website Address:

Sentence Blocks, Discussion Questions, Role Plays, Vocabulary Tests, Verb Forms Practice

Answers

Notes:

Discussion Questions:

Students have to supply their own answers to these questions. For more information see page 13.

Role Plays:

The answers produced by each pair or group of students will be different each time. For more information see page 14.

Vocabulary Tests:

The English words are provided on the vocabulary test sheets (pages 78-87). The teacher or the students have to provide the words in their first language. For more information see page 5.

Verb Forms Practice:

The answers for these pages are the same as for the sentence blocks (see below).

End of Course Examination:

The answers to the End of Course Examination are provided on the examination paper (pages 106-109). For more information see page 6.

Sentence Blocks:

Note: the last two lines of each sentence block will vary. Below there are examples given for each sentence block, but students should think of their own way to get the negative forms in the last line.

Town:

1. (Present Simple) Peter walks two kilometres to his office every day. / Who walks two kilometres to his office every day? / Peter does. / Does Peter walk two kilometres to his office every day? / Yes, he does. / Does Jeff walk two kilometres to his office every day? / No, he doesn't. Jeff doesn't walk two kilometres to his office every day.

2. (Present Continuous) We're waiting patiently for the bus at the bus stop opposite the church. / Where are you waiting patiently for the bus? / At the bus stop opposite the church. / Are you waiting patiently for the bus at the bus stop opposite the church? / Yes, we are. / Are you waiting patiently for the bus at the bus station? / No, we're not. We're not waiting patiently for the bus at the bus station.

3. (Past Simple) Jennifer bought a couple of cakes at the bakery, then ran to the post office. / What did Jennifer buy at the bakery, then run to the post office? / A couple of cakes. / Did Jennifer buy a couple of cakes at the bakery, then run to the post office? / Yes, she did. / Did Jennifer buy a loaf of bread at the bakery, then run to the post office? / No, she didn't. Jennifer didn't buy a loaf of bread at the bakery, then run to the post office.

4. (Past Continuous) The department store was opening until 10 o'clock because they were having a massive sale. / Why was the department store opening until 10 o'clock? / Because they were having a massive sale. / Was the department store opening until 10 o'clock because they were having a massive sale? / Yes, it was. / Was the department store opening until 10 o'clock because they were having staff training? / No, it wasn't. The department store wasn't opening until 10 o'clock because they were having staff training.

5. (Present Perfect) I've agreed to meet Dan in the old market place outside the library. / Who have you agreed to meet in the old market place outside the library? / Dan. / Have you agreed to meet Dan in the old market place outside the library? / Yes, I have. / Have you agreed to meet Alex in the old market place outside the library? / No, I haven't. I haven't agreed to meet Alex in the old market place outside the library.

6. (Modal Verbs) We could drive to the lake and go fishing. / Where could we drive to and go fishing? / To the lake. / Could we drive to the lake and go fishing? / Yes, we could. / Could we drive to the bowling club and go fishing? / No, we couldn't. We couldn't drive to the bowling club and go fishing.

Answers

7. (Future Forms)   The new optician's next to the bank will open next Friday. / When will the new optician's next to the bank open? / Next Friday. / Will the new optician's next to the bank open next Friday? / Yes, it will. / Will the new optician's next to the bank open next Saturday? / No, it won't. The new optician's next to the bank won't open next Saturday.

8. (First Conditional)   If the tennis court is busy we can go to the gym instead. / What can we do instead if the tennis court is busy? / Go to the gym. / Can we go to the gym instead if the tennis court is busy? / Yes, we can. / Can we go to the library instead if the tennis court is busy? / No, we can't. We can't go to the library instead if the tennis court is busy.

Food and Drink:

1. (Present Simple)   The best kind of bread is white sliced bread. / What is the best kind of bread? / White sliced bread. / Is white sliced bread the best kind of bread? / Yes, it is. / Is dry wholemeal bread the best kind of bread? / No, it isn't. Dry wholemeal bread isn't the best kind of bread.

2. (Present Continuous)   Michelle is having salad and pasta because she doesn't eat meat. / Why is Michelle having salad and pasta? / Because she doesn't eat meat. / Is Michelle having salad and pasta because she doesn't eat meat? / Yes, she is. / Is Michelle having salad and pasta because she wants to be different? / No, she isn't. Michelle isn't having salad and pasta because she wants to be different.

3. (Past Simple)   Daniel gave himself the largest portion of ice cream. / Who gave himself the largest portion of ice cream? / Daniel did. / Did Daniel give himself the largest portion of ice cream? / Yes, he did. / Did Jake give himself the largest portion of ice cream? / No, he didn't. Jake didn't give himself the largest portion of ice cream.

4. (Past Continuous)   Ellen was talking about her sister who loves fish and chips. / Who was Ellen talking about? / About her sister who loves fish and chips. / Was Ellen talking about her sister who loves fish and chips? / Yes, she was. / Was Ellen talking about her mum and dad? / No, she wasn't. Ellen wasn't talking about her mum and dad.

5. (Present Perfect)   Jenny has just put the cheese in the fridge. / Where has Jenny just put the cheese? / In the fridge. / Has Jenny just put the cheese in the fridge? / Yes, she has. / Has Jenny just put the cheese in the cupboard? / No, she hasn't. Jenny hasn't just put the cheese in the cupboard.

6. (Modal Verbs)   Potatoes can be boiled, mashed, fried, chipped, roasted, or oven-baked. / How can potatoes be prepared? / They can be boiled, mashed, fried, chipped, roasted, or oven-baked. / Can potatoes be boiled, mashed, fried, chipped, roasted, or oven-baked? / Yes, they can. / Can potatoes be eaten raw? / No, they can't. Potatoes can't be eaten raw.

7. (Future Forms)   We're going to buy some fruit at the supermarket this afternoon. / When are you going to buy some fruit at the supermarket? / This afternoon. / Are you going to buy some fruit at the supermarket this afternoon? / Yes, we are. / Are you going to buy some fruit at the supermarket this evening? / No, we're not. We're not going to buy some fruit at the supermarket this evening.

8. (First Conditional)   If you eat too much chocolate you will put on weight. / What will happen if I eat too much chocolate? / You will put on weight. / Will I put on weight if I eat too much chocolate? / Yes, you will. / Will I lose weight if I eat too much chocolate? / No, you won't. You won't lose weight if you eat too much chocolate.

Shopping:

1. (Present Simple)   Emma is the manager of a small Italian restaurant. / Who is the manager of a small Italian restaurant? / Emma is. / Is Emma the manager of a small Italian restaurant? / Yes, she is. / Is Bill the manager of a small Italian restaurant? / No, he isn't. Bill isn't the manager of a small Italian restaurant.

2. (Present Continuous)   Simon is visiting the new shopping centre near St. Mark's Road. / What is Simon doing? / Visiting the new shopping centre near St. Mark's Road. / Is Simon visiting the new shopping centre near St. Mark's Road? / Yes, he is. / Is Simon visiting the leisure centre near St. John's Road? / No, he isn't. Simon isn't visiting the leisure centre near St. John's Road.

3. (Past Simple)   I used my debit card to buy a pair of shoes for work. / What did you use to buy a pair of shoes for work? / My debit card. / Did you use your debit card to buy a pair of shoes for work? / Yes, I did. / Did you use cash to buy a pair of shoes for work? / No, I didn't. I didn't use cash to buy a pair of shoes for work.

Answers

4. (Past Continuous) Jan was leaving the car park because she had finished her shopping. / Why was Jan leaving the car park? / Because she had finished her shopping. / Was Jan leaving the car park because she had finished her shopping? / Yes, she was. / Was Jan leaving the car park because she wanted to go to the bank? / No, she wasn't. Jan wasn't leaving the car park because she wanted to go to the bank.

5. (Present Perfect) I've looked everywhere in this shop for a tin of vegetable soup, but I can't find one anywhere. / Where have you looked for a tin of vegetable soup? / Everywhere in this shop. / Have you looked everywhere in this shop for a tin of vegetable soup? / Yes, I have. / Have you looked everywhere in the supermarket next door for a tin of vegetable soup? / No, I haven't. I haven't looked everywhere in the supermarket next door for a tin of vegetable soup.

6. (Modal Verbs) We should take the lift to the fifth floor. / What should we take to the fifth floor? / The lift. / Should we take the lift to the fifth floor? / Yes, we should. / Should we take the stairs to the fifth floor? / No, we shouldn't. We shouldn't take the stairs to the fifth floor.

7. (Future Forms) After we finish buying groceries we'll go to Nero's for a quick coffee. / When will we go to Nero's for a quick coffee? / After we finish buying groceries. / Will we go to Nero's for a quick coffee after we finish buying groceries? / Yes, we will. / Will we go to Nero's for a quick coffee in a minute? / No, we won't. We won't go to Nero's for a quick coffee in a minute.

8. (First Conditional) If the checkout assistant offers to pack my bags I'll let her. / What will you do if the checkout assistant offers to pack your bags? / Let her. / Will you let her if the checkout assistant offers to pack your bags? / Yes, I will. / Will you stop her if the checkout assistant offers to pack your bags? / No, I won't. I won't stop her if the checkout assistant offers to pack my bags.

Health:

1. (Present Simple) Being healthy is very important to me. / What is very important to you? / Being healthy. / Is being healthy very important to you? / Yes, it is. / Is being successful very important to you? / No, it isn't. Being successful isn't very important to me.

2. (Present Continuous) Sammi is sitting in the waiting room with her mum and brother. / Where is Sammi sitting with her mum and brother? / In the waiting room. / Is Sammi sitting in the waiting room with her mum and brother? / Yes, she is. / Is Sammi sitting in the doctor's office with her mum and brother? / No, she isn't. Sammi isn't sitting in the doctor's office with her mum and brother.

3. (Past Simple) I phoned my doctor this morning to make an appointment. / Why did you phone your doctor this morning? / To make an appointment. / Did you phone your doctor this morning to make an appointment? / Yes, I did. / Did you phone your doctor this morning to find out the results of your blood test? / No, I didn't. I didn't phone my doctor this morning to find out the results of my blood test.

4. (Past Continuous) Ella was telling the receptionist about her husband's painful arthritis. / Who was telling the receptionist about her husband's painful arthritis? / Ella was. / Was Ella telling the receptionist about her husband's painful arthritis? / Yes, she was. / Was Joanne telling the receptionist about her husband's painful arthritis? / No, she wasn't. Joanne wasn't telling the receptionist about her husband's painful arthritis.

5. (Present Perfect) I've taken two tablets three times a day for a week, but I still don't feel any better. / How many tablets have you taken three times a day for a week? / Two. / Have you taken two tablets three times a day for a week? / Yes, I have. / Have you taken three tablets three times a day for a week? / No, I haven't. I haven't taken three tablets three times a day for a week.

6. (Modal Verbs) Kenny has to take his prescription to the pharmacy tomorrow. / When does Kenny have to take his prescription to the pharmacy? / Tomorrow. / Does Kenny have to take his prescription to the pharmacy tomorrow? / Yes, he does. / Does Kenny have to take his prescription to the pharmacy next Monday? No, he doesn't. Kenny doesn't have to take his prescription to the pharmacy next Monday.

7. (Future Forms) Simon is going to visit the optician's for an eye examination. / Why is Simon going to visit the optician's? / For an eye examination. / Is Simon going to visit the optician's for an eye examination? / Yes, he is. / Is Simon going to visit the optician's for an operation? / No, he isn't. Simon isn't going to visit the optician's for an operation.

8. (First Conditional) If you ask the doctor she will give you some good advice about your problem. / What will happen if I ask the doctor about my problem? / She will give you some good advice. / Will the doctor give me some

Answers

good advice about my problem if I ask her? / Yes, she will. / Will the doctor give me some unhelpful advice about my problem if I ask her? / No, she won't. The doctor won't give you some unhelpful advice about your problem if you ask her.

Transport:

1. (Present Simple)   I usually get the train at 7.28. / When do you usually get the train? / At 7.28. / Do you usually get the train at 7.28? / Yes, I do. / Do you usually get the train at 7.48? / No, I don't. I don't usually get the train at 7.48.

2. (Present Continuous)   Gemma is driving to the airport to pick up her grandmother. / Where is Gemma driving to? / To the airport to pick up her grandmother. / Is Gemma driving to the airport to pick up her grandmother? / Yes, she is. / Is Gemma driving to Manchester to go shopping? / No, she isn't. Gemma isn't driving to Manchester to go shopping.

3. (Past Simple)   I flew from Heathrow to Copenhagen last night. / What did you do last night? / I flew from Heathrow to Copenhagen. / Did you fly from Heathrow to Copenhagen last night? / Yes, I did. / Did you go to the cinema last night? / No, I didn't. I didn't go to the cinema last night.

4. (Past Continuous)   Oliver was crossing the road when he was hit by a bus. / Who was crossing the road when he was hit by a bus? / Oliver was. / Was Oliver crossing the road when he was hit by a bus? / Yes, he was. / Was Anne crossing the road when she was hit by a bus? / No, she wasn't. Anne wasn't crossing the road when she was hit by a bus.

5. (Present Perfect)   We've cancelled our flight because our daughter is ill. / Why have you cancelled your flight? / Because our daughter is ill. / Have you cancelled your flight because your daughter is ill? / Yes, we have. / Have you cancelled your flight because you can't get time off work? / No, we haven't. We haven't cancelled our flight because we can't get time off work.

6. (Modal Verbs)   All passengers must show their passports and boarding passes at the gate. / What must all passengers show at the gate? / Their passports and boarding passes. / Must all passengers show their passports and boarding passes at the gate? / Yes, they must. / Must all passengers show their holiday photos and souvenirs at the gate? / No, they mustn't. All passengers mustn't show their holiday photos and souvenirs at the gate.

7. (Future Forms)   The next train to arrive at platform 8 will be the 9.49 service to Cardiff. / Which train will be the next to arrive at platform 8? / The 9.49 service to Cardiff. / Will the next train to arrive at platform 8 be the 9.49 service to Cardiff? / Yes, it will. / Will the next train to arrive at platform 8 be the 10.21 service to Lincoln? / No, it won't. The next train to arrive at platform 8 won't be the 10.21 service to Lincoln.

8. (First Conditional)   If we cycle to work we'll get there in about an hour. / When will we get there if we cycle to work? / In about an hour. / Will we get there in about an hour if we cycle to work? / Yes, we will. / Will we get there in under an hour if we cycle to work? / No, we won't. We won't get there in under an hour if we cycle to work.

Family:

1. (Present Simple)   My mum lives with her new partner in Brighton. / Where does your mum live? / With her new partner in Brighton. / Does your mum live with her new partner in Brighton? / Yes, she does. / Does you mum live with her new partner in Aberdeen? / No, she doesn't. My mum doesn't live with her new partner in Aberdeen.

2. (Present Continuous)   Roberto's daughter is playing with her cousins. / What is Roberto's daughter doing? / Playing with her cousins. / Is Roberto's daughter playing with her cousins? / Yes, she is. / Is Roberto's daughter watching TV with her cousins? / No, she isn't. Roberto's daughter isn't watching TV with her cousins.

3. (Past Simple)   Jenna's aunt and uncle visited us in May because they wanted to see our new baby. / Why did Jenna's aunt and uncle visit you in May? / Because they wanted to see our new baby. Did Jenna's aunt and uncle visit you in May because they wanted to see your new baby? / Yes, they did. / Did Jenna's aunt and uncle visit you in May because they wanted to see your new house? / No, they didn't. Jenna's aunt and uncle didn't visit us in May because they wanted to see our new house.

4. (Past Continuous)   My sister was walking to the city museum with her children when she saw a fox. / Where was your sister walking to with her children when she saw a fox? / To the city museum. / Was your sister walking to the city museum with her children when she saw a fox? / Yes, she was. / Was your sister walking to the bank with her

Answers

children when she saw a fox? / No, she wasn't. My sister wasn't walking to the bank with her children when she saw a fox.

5. (Present Perfect)   The whole family has decided to go on holiday to Florida next year. / Who has decided to go on holiday to Florida next year? / The whole family has. / Has the whole family decided to go on holiday to Florida next year? / Yes, it has. / Has your best friend decided to go on holiday to Florida next year? / No, she hasn't. My best friend hasn't decided to go on holiday to Florida next year.

6. (Modal Verbs)   Your grandma and granddad should think about moving into a retirement bungalow. / Whose grandma and granddad should think about moving into a retirement bungalow? / Your grandma and granddad. / Should my grandma and granddad think about moving into a retirement bungalow? / Yes, they should. / Should my friend's grandma and granddad think about moving into a retirement bungalow? / No, they shouldn't. My friend's grandma and granddad shouldn't think about moving into a retirement bungalow.

7. (Future Forms)   Sam's brother is going to start university in Edinburgh next September. / When is Sam's brother going to start university in Edinburgh? / Next September. / Is Sam's brother going to start university in Edinburgh next September? / Yes, he is. / Is Sam's brother going to start university in Edinburgh next January? / No, he isn't. Sam's brother isn't going to start university in Edinburgh next January.

8. (First Conditional)   If our parents get divorced the family will be very disappointed. / What will happen if your parents get divorced? / The family will be very disappointed. / Will the family be very disappointed if your parents get divorced? / Yes, it will. / Will the family be very pleased if your parents get divorced? / No, it won't. The family won't be very pleased if our parents get divorced.

Clothes:

1. (Present Simple)   I wear glasses because I'm short-sighted. / Why do you wear glasses? / Because I'm short-sighted. / Do you wear glasses because you're short-sighted? / Yes, I do. / Do you wear glasses because you like wearing them? / No, I don't. I don't wear glasses because I like wearing them.

2. (Present Continuous)   Harry is trying on a new pair of smart black trousers. / Who is trying on a new pair of smart black trousers? / Harry is. / Is Harry trying on a new pair of smart black trousers? / Yes, he is. / Is Darren trying on a new pair of smart black trousers? / No, he isn't. Darren isn't trying on a new pair of smart black trousers.

3. (Past Simple)   Frankie bought herself a new dress and some underwear in the trendiest boutique on Oxford Street. / Where did Frankie buy herself a new dress and some underwear? / In the trendiest boutique on Oxford Street. / Did Frankie buy herself a new dress and some underwear in the trendiest boutique on Oxford Street? / Yes, she did. / Did Frankie buy herself a new dress and some underwear in a supermarket in Crawley? / No, she didn't. Frankie didn't buy herself a new dress and some underwear in a supermarket in Crawley.

4. (Past Continuous)   Michael was wearing the yellow and brown striped pyjamas that his grandma had knitted him for Christmas. / Who was wearing the yellow and brown striped pyjamas that his grandma had knitted him for Christmas? / Michael was. / Was Michael wearing the yellow and brown striped pyjamas that his grandma had knitted him for Christmas? / Yes, he was. / Was Paul wearing the yellow and brown striped pyjamas that his grandma had knitted him for Christmas? / No, he wasn't. Paul wasn't wearing the yellow and brown striped pyjamas that his grandma had knitted him for Christmas.

5. (Present Perfect)   I have always liked jackets and tops from Marks and Spencer. / What have you always liked? / Jackets and tops from Marks and Spencer. / Have you always liked jackets and tops from Marks and Spencer? / Yes, I have. / Have you always liked jackets and tops from ASDA? / No, I haven't. I haven't always liked jackets and tops from ASDA.

6. (Modal Verbs)   Stephen has to wear a blue and grey uniform every day for his job as a security guard. / When does Stephen have to wear a blue and grey uniform for his job as a security guard? / Every day. / Does Stephen have to wear a blue and grey uniform every day for his job as a security guard? / Yes, he does. / Does Stephen have to wear a blue and grey uniform once a week for his job as a security guard? / No, he doesn't. Stephen doesn't have to wear a blue and grey uniform once a week for his job as a security guard.

7. (Future Forms)   We'll have a clearout of our wardrobe to see what we can give away to charity. / Why will we have a clearout of our wardrobe? / To see what we can give away to charity. / Will we have a clearout of our wardrobe to see what we can give away to charity? / Yes, we will. / Will we have a clearout of our wardrobe because we want to tidy up? / No, we won't. We won't have a clearout of our wardrobe because we want to tidy up.

Answers

8. (First Conditional) If you wear a suit and tie to the interview you'll make an excellent impression. / What kind of impression will I make if I wear a suit and tie to the interview? / An excellent one. / Will I make an excellent impression if I wear a suit and tie to the interview? / Yes, you will. / Will I make a bad impression if I wear a suit and tie to the interview? / No, you won't. You won't make a bad impression if you wear a suit and tie to the interview.

Work:

1. (Present Simple) Gerry hates working part-time for his dad's furniture business. / Who hates working part-time for his dad's furniture business? / Gerry does. / Does Gerry hate working part-time for his dad's furniture business? / Yes, he does. / Does Joanna hate working part-time for her dad's furniture business? / No, she doesn't. Joanna doesn't hate working part-time for her dad's furniture business.

2. (Present Continuous) Helena is hoping to get promoted at the end of the year. / When is Helena hoping to get promoted? / At the end of the year. / Is Helena hoping to get promoted at the end of the year? / Yes, she is. / Is Helena hoping to get promoted next March? / No, she isn't. Helena isn't hoping to get promoted next March.

3. (Past Simple) When Greg worked for Dell he had to do plenty of overtime. / What did Greg have to do when he worked for Dell? / Plenty of overtime. / Did Greg have to do plenty of overtime when he worked for Dell? / Yes, he did. / Did Greg have to take a pay cut when he worked for Dell? / No, he didn't. Greg didn't have to take a pay cut when he worked for Dell.

4. (Past Continuous) Edward was updating his CV because he wanted to apply for a new job. / Why was Edward updating his CV? / Because he wanted to apply for a new job. / Was Edward updating his CV because he wanted to apply for a new job? / Yes, he was. / Was Edward updating his CV because he was happy in his job? / No, he wasn't. Edward wasn't updating his CV because he was happy in his job.

5. (Present Perfect) My friend Jo has been unemployed since last August. / How long has your friend Jo been unemployed for? / Since last August. / Has your friend Jo been unemployed since last August? / Yes, she has. / Has your friend Jo been unemployed for eight months? / No, she hasn't. My friend Jo hasn't been unemployed for eight months.

6. (Modal Verbs) You need to ask your manager for a pay rise as soon as possible! / What do I need to ask my manager for as soon as possible? / For a pay rise. / Do I need to ask my manager for a pay rise as soon as possible? / Yes, you do. / Do I need to ask my manager for more work as soon as possible? / No, you don't. You don't need to ask your manager for more work as soon as possible.

7. (Future Forms) I'm going to visit that new employment agency about temporary work. / Where are you going to visit about temporary work? / That new employment agency. / Are you going to visit that new employment agency about temporary work? / Yes, I am. / Are you going to visit the betting shop about temporary work? / No, I'm not. I'm not going to visit the betting shop about temporary work.

8. (First Conditional) Dave will have to work very hard if he wants to have a successful career in sales. / What will Dave have to do if he wants to have a successful career in sales? / Work very hard. / Will Dave have to work very hard if he wants to have a successful career in sales? / Yes, he will. / Will Dave have to work part-time if he wants to have a successful career in sales? / No, he won't. Dave won't have to work part-time if he wants to have a successful career in sales.

Home:

1. (Present Simple) I live in a small semi-detached house in Manchester. / Where do you live? / In a small semi-detached house in Manchester. / Do you live in a small semi-detached house in Manchester? / Yes, I do. / Do you live in a large detached house in Wimbledon? / No, I don't. I don't live in a large detached house in Wimbledon.

2. (Present Continuous) Mark is buying a new washing machine because his old one is broken. / Why is Mark buying a new washing machine? / Because his old one is broken. / Is Mark buying a new washing machine because his old one is broken? / Yes, he is. / Is Mark buying a new washing machine because he would like to own two washing machines? / No, he isn't. Mark isn't buying a new washing machine because he would like to own two washing machines.

3. (Past Simple) When I went to their home Jack and Lisa showed me their new bathroom. / What did Jack and Lisa show you when you went to their home? / Their new bathroom. / Did Jack and Lisa show you their new bathroom when you went to their home? / Yes, they did. / Did Jack and Lisa show you their new widescreen plasma

Answers

TV when you went to their home? / No, they didn't. Jack and Lisa didn't show me their new widescreen plasma TV when I went to their home.

4. (Past Continuous)   Sarah and Noel were watching funny DVDs in their living room for three hours last night. / Who was watching funny DVDs in their living room for three hours last night? / Sarah and Noel were. / Were Sarah and Noel watching funny DVDs in their living room for three hours last night? / Yes, they were. / Were Stu and Kylie watching funny DVDs in their living room for three hours last night? / No, they weren't. Stu and Kylie weren't watching funny DVDs in their living room for three hours last night.

5. (Present Perfect)   Jason has finished cutting the grass in the back garden. / What has Jason finished doing in the back garden? / Cutting the grass. / Has Jason finished cutting the grass in the back garden? / Yes, he has. / Has Jason finished watering the plants in the back garden? / No, he hasn't. Jason hasn't finished watering the plants in the back garden.

6. (Modal Verbs)   Barry has to do the washing up every night after tea. / How often does Barry have to do the washing up? / Every night after tea. / Does Barry have to do the washing up every night after tea? / Yes, he does. / Does Barry have to do the washing up every morning after breakfast? / No, he doesn't. Barry doesn't have to do the washing up every morning after breakfast.

7. (Future Forms)   I'll do the hoovering quickly before I have a bath. / When will you do the hoovering? / Before I have a bath. / Will you do the hoovering quickly before you have a bath? / Yes, I will. / Will you do the hoovering quickly after you have a bath? / No, I won't. I won't do the hoovering quickly after I have a bath.

8. (First Conditional)   If you sell your horrible flat you'll be able to put down a deposit on a nice house. / What will I be able to do if I sell my horrible flat? / Put down a deposit on a nice house. / Will I be able to put down a deposit on a nice house if I sell my horrible flat? / Yes, you will. / Will I be able to buy a nice house without a mortgage if I sell my horrible flat? / No, you won't. You won't be able to buy a nice house without a mortgage if you sell your horrible flat.

Free Time:

1. (Present Simple)   I love going to the cinema with my friends, because we always have a good time. / Why do you love going to the cinema with your friends? / Because we always have a good time. / Do you love going to the cinema with your friends because you always have a good time? / Yes, I do. / Do you love going to the cinema with your friends because you like walking to the cinema? / No, I don't. I don't love going to the cinema with my friends because I like walking to the cinema.

2. (Present Continuous)   Barney and Wanda are enjoying a day out at an amusement park. / Who is enjoying a day out at an amusement park? / Barney and Wanda are. / Are Barney and Wanda enjoying a day out at an amusement park? / Yes, they are. / Are Alex and Sue enjoying a day out at an amusement park? / No, they aren't. Alex and Sue aren't enjoying a day out at an amusement park.

3. (Past Simple)   We went on a camping holiday last summer for two weeks. / How long did you go on a camping holiday for last summer? / For two weeks. / Did you go on a camping holiday last summer for two weeks? / Yes, we did. / Did you go on a camping holiday last summer for a week? / No, we didn't. We didn't go on a camping holiday last summer for a week.

4. (Past Continuous)   Chester's son was playing golf badly yesterday afternoon with a few friends from his cousin's bowling club. / How was Chester's son playing golf yesterday afternoon with a few friends from his cousin's bowling club? / Badly. / Was Chester's son playing golf badly yesterday afternoon with a few friends from his cousin's bowling club? / Yes, he was. / Was Chester's son playing golf well yesterday afternoon with a few friends from his cousin's bowling club? / No, he wasn't. Chester's son wasn't playing golf well yesterday afternoon with a few friends from his cousin's bowling club.

5. (Present Perfect)   I have seen Macbeth at this theatre five times. / How many times have you seen Macbeth at this theatre? / Five times. / Have you seen Macbeth at this theatre five times? / Yes, I have. / Have you seen Macbeth at this theatre six times? / No, I haven't. I haven't seen Macbeth at this theatre six times.

6. (Modal Verbs)   You should do some exercise instead of playing computer games all day. / What should I do instead of playing computer games all day? / Some exercise. / Should I do some exercise instead of playing computer games all day? / Yes, you should. / Should I watch TV instead of playing computer games all day? / No, you shouldn't. You shouldn't watch TV instead of playing computer games all day.

Answers

7. (Future Forms) Me, Jess and Casey are going to watch the tennis in the park. / Where are you, Jess and Casey going to watch the tennis? / In the park. / Are you, Jess and Casey going to watch the tennis in the park? / Yes, we are. / Are you, Jess and Casey going to watch the tennis at the playing field? / No, we're not. Me, Jess and Casey are not going to watch the tennis at the playing field.

8. (First Conditional) If the leisure centre is still open we can all go swimming. / What can we all do if the leisure centre is still open? / Go swimming. / Can we all go swimming if the leisure centre is still open? / Yes, we can. / Can we all have a fight there if the leisure centre is still open? / No, we can't. We can't all have a fight there if the leisure centre is still open.

Sentence Block Extensions:

There isn't room in this book to print in full all of the 231 sentence blocks from the extensions pages (on pages 30-33). We hope that the answers given above will give you the teacher (or you the student) enough guidance to be able to make the sentence block extensions in this book confidently. For all of the sentence block starting sentences there are at least two different wh- question words that can be used to make sentence blocks. In some cases as many as 6 or 7 different sentence blocks can be made from the same starting sentence when using different wh- question words. For example, let's look at the first starting sentence from the "Town" unit:

Peter walks two kilometres to his office every day.

On the handout the wh- question word that is given is "Who", but this starting sentence also works equally well with four other wh- questions: "What", "Where", "When", and "How far":

What does Peter do every day? / Peter walks two kilometres to his office.

Where does Peter walk two kilometres to every day? / To his office.

When does Peter walk two kilometres to his office? / Every day.

How far does Peter walk to his office every day? / Two kilometres.

The idea is easy. Change the wh- question word each time and the students can make five completely different sentence blocks from the original starting sentence, simply by finding the relevant information for the answer in the starting sentence. Sometimes the same wh- question word can be used more than once to make different sentence blocks, as with this example from the "Transport" unit: I usually get the train at 7.28.

What do you usually get at 7.28?
What do you usually do at 7.28?
What time do you usually get the train?

If your students are getting to grips with making sentence blocks and are keen to do more than the eight given on the handout each week, ask them to study some of the starting sentences and work out whether or not other wh- question words could be used to form new sentence blocks; or simply give them the sentence block extension pages and let them try to form all the possible sentence blocks that exist for each starting sentence.

Discussion Words and Question Sheets:

Town:

General Questions:

1. Answers will vary.

2. Answers will vary.

3. a) 7 words have 1 syllable: bank, church, mosque, school, town, lake, bridge. b) 13 words have 2 syllables: pavement, office, bookshop, bus stop, clothes shop, library, river, building, chemist, college, village, town hall, city.

Answers

c) 11 words have 3 syllables: bakery, optician's, building site, post office, casino, cathedral, tennis court, traffic lights, market place, car showroom, tax office. d) 5 words have 4 syllables: bed and breakfast, apartment block, department store, police station, public toilets. e) 3 words have 5 syllables: football stadium, university, holiday resort. f) 1 word has 6 syllables: community centre.

4. 2 syllable words: all of the words have the strong stress on the first syllable: **pave**ment, **off**ice, **book**shop, **bus** stop, **clothes** shop, **lib**rary, **ri**ver, **buil**ding, **che**mist, **col**lege, **vill**age, **town** hall, **ci**ty. 3 syllable words: these words have the strong stress on the first syllable: **bak**ery, **buil**ding site, **post** office, **ten**nis court, **traff**ic lights, **mar**ket place, **tax** office; these words have the strong stress on the middle syllable: op**ti**cian's, ca**si**no, ca**the**dral, car **show**room. 4 syllable words: these words have the strong stress on the second syllable: a**part**ment block, de**part**ment store, po**lice** station; these words have the strong stress on the third syllable: bed and **break**fast, public **toi**lets. 5 syllable words: these words have the strong stress on the first syllable: **foot**ball stadium, **ho**liday resort; this word has the strong stress on the third syllable: uni**ver**sity. 6 syllable word: this word has the strong stress on the second syllable: com**mu**nity centre.

5. Apartment block, bakery, bank, bed and breakfast, bookshop, bridge, building, building site, bus stop, car showroom, casino, cathedral, chemist, church, city, clothes shop, college, community centre, department store, football stadium, holiday resort, lake, library, market place, mosque, office, optician's, pavement, police station, post office, public toilets, river, school, tax office, tennis court, town, town hall, traffic lights, university, village.

6. 4 letters: bank, city, lake, town. 5 letters: river. 6 letters: bakery, bridge, casino, church, mosque, office, school. 7 letters: bus stop, chemist, college, library, village. 8 letters: bookshop, building, pavement, town hall. 9 letters: cathedral, optician's, tax office. 10 letters: post office, university. 11 letters: car showroom, clothes shop, market place, tennis court. 12 letters: building site. 13 letters: holiday resort, police station, public toilets, traffic lights. 14 letters: apartment block, football stadium. 15 letters: bed and breakfast, community centre, department store.

7. See answer to number 5 above.

8. Answers will vary.

Lesson Questions:

1. Optician's.

2. a) and b) The places where I could buy something, and what I could buy at each place (answers for the latter will vary) are: bakery (bread rolls, bread, cakes), bank (loan, mortgage), bookshop (book, notebook, calendar), optician's (glasses, contact lenses), clothes shop (jumper, jacket, shoes), football stadium (season ticket, hot dog), post office (stamps, envelopes, birthday card), casino (chips), library (second hand books, time on the internet), tennis court (tennis lessons), department store (furniture, clothes, electrical goods), market place (clothes, cleaning products, second hand books, CDs and DVDs), chemist (medicine, tablets, cough sweets), university (course, course books), car showroom (car, car polish), holiday resort (drinks, meals, hotel room). Five more kinds of shop are: delicatessen (pastries, mayonnaise), butcher's (meat, fish), jeweller's (ring, watch), supermarket (groceries, DVDs), DIY store (bath tiles, paint).

3. Bakery.

4. School, community centre, university, college.

5. Church, mosque, cathedral.

6. Holiday resort.

7. Building site.

8. River, lake.

9. Football stadium, tennis court, university.

10. Casino.

11. Chemist.

12. Library.

Answers

13. Bank.

14. From smallest to largest: village, town, city.

Food and Drink:

General Questions:

1. Answers will vary.

2. Answers will vary.

3. a) 19 words have 1 syllable: milk, rice, soup, bread, fruit, meal, wine, crisps, cheese, lamb, nut, meat, fish, flour, egg, pie, chips, food, beef. b) 13 words have 2 syllables: carrot, orange, pizza, sausage, onion, butter, fruit juice, chocolate, chicken, apple, pasta, water, mushroom. c) 7 words have 3 syllables: tomato, banana, cereal, potato, lemonade, vegetable, strawberry. d) 1 word has 4 syllables: mineral water.

4. 2 syllable words: all of the words have the strong stress on the first syllable: **ca**rrot, **o**range, **pi**zza, **sau**sage, **on**ion, **but**ter, **fruit** juice, **choc**olate, **chi**cken, **a**pple, **pa**sta, **wa**ter, **mush**room. 3 syllable words: these words have the strong stress on the first syllable: **ce**real, **ve**getable, **straw**berry; these words have the strong stress on the middle syllable: to**ma**to, ba**na**na, po**ta**to; this word has the strong stress on the last syllable: lemon**ade**. 4 syllable words: this word has the strong stress on the first syllable: **min**eral water.

5. Apple, banana, beef, bread, butter, carrot, cereal, cheese, chicken, chips, chocolate, crisps, egg, fish, flour, food, fruit, fruit juice, lamb, lemonade, meal, meat, milk, mineral water, mushroom, nut, onion, orange, pasta, pie, pizza, potato, rice, sausage, soup, strawberry, tomato, vegetable, water, wine.

6. 3 letters: egg, nut, pie. 4 letters: beef, fish, food, lamb, meal, meat, milk, rice, soup, wine. 5 letters: apple, bread, chips, flour, fruit, onion, pasta, pizza, water. 6 letters: banana, butter, carrot, cereal, cheese, crisps, orange, potato, tomato. 7 letters: chicken, sausage. 8 letters: lemonade, mushroom. 9 letters: chocolate, vegetable. 10 letters: fruit juice, strawberry. 12 letters: mineral water.

7. See answer to number 5 above.

8. Answers will vary.

Lesson Questions:

1. Answers will vary.

2. Carrot, tomato, onion, mushroom. Answers will vary – five more vegetables could be: leek, cabbage, cucumber, lettuce, beetroot.

3. Pizza and pasta.

4. Milk, mineral water, wine, lemonade, fruit juice, water. Answers will vary – five more drinks could be: cola, coffee, tea, beer, orange squash.

5. Egg.

6. Orange, banana, apple, strawberry. Answers will vary – five more fruits could be: apricot, peach, raspberry, pear, grapes.

7. Chips.

8. Answers will vary. Suggested answers: a) butter, cheese, chips, chocolate, crisps, lemonade, nut, pie, pizza, wine. b) apple, banana, cereal, carrot, fish, fruit, fruit juice, milk, mineral water, mushroom, onion, orange, strawberry, tomato, vegetable, water.

9. Bread.

10. Milk.

Answers

11. Nut.

12. Wine.

13. Lamb, fish, chicken, beef. b) Answers will vary.

14. Cheese.

Shopping:

General Questions:

1. Answers will vary.

2. Answers will vary.

3. a) 15 words have 1 syllable: aisle, cash, price, till, sale, scales, change, queue, pence, shelf, bag, lift, pounds, bench, shop. b) 10 words have 2 syllables: car park, market, way in, trolley, checkout, cash point, receipt, way out, refund, money. c) 9 words have 3 syllables: local shop, customer, groceries, debit card, promotion, restaurant, express lane, manager, frozen food. d) 4 words have 4 syllables: supermarket, shopping centre, escalator, opening times. e) 2 words have 5 syllables: checkout assistant, delicatessen.

4. 2 syllable words: these words have the strong stress on the first syllable: **car** park, **mar**ket, **trol**ley, **check**out, **cash** point, **re**fund, **mo**ney; these words have the strong stress on the second syllable: way **in**, re**ceipt**, way **out**. 3 syllable words: these words have the strong stress on the first syllable: **cus**tomer, **gro**ceries, **de**bit card, **res**taurant, **ma**nager; these words have the strong stress on the middle syllable: pro**mo**tion, ex**press** lane; these words have the strong stress on the last syllable: local **shop**, frozen **food**. 4 syllable words: all of the words have the strong stress on the first syllable: **su**permarket, **sho**pping centre, **es**calator, **o**pening times. 5 syllable words: this word has the strong stress on the first syllable: **che**ckout assistant; this word has the strong stress on the fourth syllable: delica**tes**sen.

5. Aisle, bag, bench, car park, cash, cash point, change, checkout, checkout assistant, customer, debit card, delicatessen, escalator, express lane, frozen food, groceries, lift, local shop, manager, market, money, opening times, pence, pounds, price, promotion, receipt, queue, refund, restaurant, sale, scales, shelf, shop, shopping centre, supermarket, till, trolley, way in, way out.

6. 3 letters: bag. 4 letters: cash, lift, sale, shop, till. 5 letters: aisle, bench, money, pence, price, queue, shelf, way in. 6 letters: change, market, pounds, refund, scales, way out. 7 letters: car park, manager, receipt, trolley. 8 letters: checkout, customer. 9 letters: cash point, debit card, escalator, groceries, local shop, promotion. 10 letters: restaurant, frozen food. 11 letters: supermarket, express lane. 12 letters: delicatessen, opening times. 14 letters: shopping centre. 17 letters: checkout assistant.

7. See answer to number 5 above.

8. Answers will vary.

Lesson Questions:

1. Groceries.

2. Cash, debit card, change, pence, pounds, money. Answers will vary – you could also pay with a credit card.

3. Trolley.

4. Checkout assistant.

5. Refund.

6. Way in.

7. Restaurant.

8. Change, receipt.

Answers

9. Delicatessen.

10. Lift.

11. Sale.

12. Bench.

13. Scales.

14. Customer.

Health:

General Questions:

1. Answers will vary.

2. Answers will vary.

3. a) 6 words have 1 syllable: bruise, cut, health, crutch, nurse, rash. b) 17 words have 2 syllables: toothbrush, illness, stretcher, toothpaste, cancer, dentist, stitches, headache, fever, tablets, x-ray, doctor, plaster, wheelchair, patient, problem, needle. c) 14 words have 3 syllables: infection, stomach ache, pharmacy, surgery, stethoscope, broken bone, hospital, injection, waiting room, ambulance, appointment, prescription, allergy, accident. d) 2 words have 4 syllables: emergency, receptionist. e) 1 word has 5 syllables: examination.

4. 2 syllable words: all of the words have the strong stress on the first syllable: **tooth**brush, **ill**ness, **stret**cher, **tooth**paste, **can**cer, **den**tist, **stit**ches, **head**ache, **fe**ver, **tab**lets, **x**-ray, **doc**tor, **plas**ter, **wheel**chair, **pa**tient, **prob**lem, **nee**dle. 3 syllable words: these words have the strong stress on the first syllable: **sto**mach ache, **phar**macy, **sur**gery, **steth**oscope, **hos**pital, **wait**ing room, **am**bulance, **all**ergy, **acc**ident; these words have the strong stress on the middle syllable: in**fec**tion, in**jec**tion, ap**point**ment, pre**scrip**tion; this word has the strong stress on the last syllable: broken **bone**. 4 syllable words: both words have the strong stress on the second syllable: e**mer**gency, re**cep**tionist. 5 syllable word: this word has the strong stress on the fourth syllable: exami**na**tion.

5. accident, allergy, ambulance, appointment, broken bone, bruise, cancer, crutch, cut, dentist, doctor, emergency, examination, fever, headache, health, hospital, illness, infection, injection, needle, nurse, patient, pharmacy, plaster, prescription, problem, rash, receptionist, stethoscope, stitches, stomach ache, stretcher, surgery, tablets, toothbrush, toothpaste, waiting room, wheelchair, x-ray.

6. 3 letters: cut. 4 letters: rash, x-ray. 5 letters: fever, nurse. 6 letters: bruise, cancer, crutch, doctor, health, needle. 7 letters: allergy, dentist, illness, patient, plaster, problem, surgery, tablets. 8 letters: accident, headache, hospital, pharmacy, stitches. 9 letters: ambulance, emergency, infection, injection, stretcher. 10 letters: broken bone, toothbrush, toothpaste, wheelchair. 11 letters: appointment, examination, stethoscope, stomach ache, waiting room. 12 letters: prescription, receptionist.

7. See answer to number 5 above.

8. Answers will vary.

Lesson Questions:

1. Answers will vary. Suggested answer: rash, bruise, cut, headache, stomach ache, infection, allergy, fever, broken bone, cancer.

2. Wheelchair.

3. Emergency.

4. Injection.

5. Fever.

Answers

6. X-ray.

7. 4 words: examination, infection, injection, prescription.

8. Ambulance.

9. a) Nurse, b) health, c) bruise, d) rash, e) fever, f) crutch.

10. Dentist, toothbrush, toothpaste.

11. Tablets.

12. Answers will vary. Suggested answer: ambulance (lie down), hospital (visit a friend), pharmacy (buy some medicine), waiting room (wait to see your doctor).

13. Appointment.

14. Stethoscope.

Transport:

General Questions:

1. Answers will vary.

2. Answers will vary.

3. a) 13 words have 1 syllable: fare, tyre, boat, bus, fine, cruise, train, car, bike, road, ship, flight, van. b) 15 words have 2 syllables: ticket, take-off, canoe, station, driver, engine, ferry, tractor, taxi, car park, road sign, airport, garage, runway, journey. c) 7 words have 3 syllables: petrol pump, motorway, passenger, commuter, aeroplane, motorbike, roundabout. d) 4 words have 4 syllables: cancellation, driving licence, reservation, service station. e) 1 word has 6 syllables: emergency exit.

4. 2 syllable words: all of the words have the strong stress on the first syllable, apart from can**oe**: **ti**cket, **take**-off, **sta**tion, **dri**ver, **en**gine, **fe**rry, **trac**tor, **ta**xi, **car** park, **road** sign, **air**port, **ga**rage, **run**way, **jour**ney. 3 syllable words: these words have the strong stress on the first syllable: **pe**trol pump, **mo**torway, **pass**enger, **ae**roplane, **mo**torbike, **round**about; this word has the strong stress on the middle syllable: com**mu**ter. 4 syllable words: these words have the strong stress on the first syllable: **dri**ving licence, **ser**vice station; these words have the strong stress on the third syllable: cancel**la**tion, reser**va**tion. 6 syllable word: this word has the strong stress on the fifth syllable: emergency **ex**it.

5. Aeroplane, airport, bike, boat, bus, cancellation, canoe, car, car park, commuter, cruise, driver, driving licence, emergency exit, engine, fare, ferry, fine, flight, garage, journey, motorbike, motorway, passenger, petrol pump, reservation, road, roundabout, runway, sign, service station, ship, station, taxi, ticket, take-off, tractor, train, tyre, van.

6. 3 letters: bus, car, van. 4 letters: bike, boat, fare, fine, road, ship, sign, taxi, tyre. 5 letters: canoe, ferry, train. 6 letters: cruise, driver, engine, flight, garage, runway, ticket. 7 letters: airport, car park, journey, station, take-off, tractor. 8 letters: commuter, motorway. 9 letters: aeroplane, motorbike, passenger. 10 letters: petrol pump, roundabout. 11 letters: reservation. 12 letters: cancellation. 13 letters: emergency exit. 14 letters: driving licence, service station.

7. See answer to number 5 above.

8. Answers will vary.

Lesson Questions:

1. Driving licence.

2. Boat, bus, canoe, train, aeroplane, ferry, tractor, car, taxi, bike, ship, motorbike, van.

3. Petrol pump.

Complete 12-week Spoken English Course

Answers

4. Cancellation.

5. Service station.

6. Answers will vary.

7. a) Boat, b) bus, c) ferry, d) tyre, e) fare, f) bike.

8. Passenger.

9. Answers will vary. Suggested answer: tractor, canoe, bike, bus, van, car, taxi, motorbike, boat, ferry, ship, train, aeroplane.

10. Car park.

11. Tractor.

12. Fare.

13. a) Van, tractor, car, taxi, bike, motorbike, bus, b) boat, canoe, ship, ferry, c) train, d) aeroplane. Answers to the second part of the question will vary. Suggested answers: a) tandem, b) dinghy, c) tram, d) helicopter.

14. Take-off.

Family:

General Questions:

1. Answers will vary.

2. Answers will vary.

3. a) 11 words have 1 syllable: son, girl, niece, child, dad, mum, ex-, aunt, man, boy, wife. b) 19 words have 2 syllables: boyfriend, mother, grandchild, granddad, grandma, nephew, uncle, woman, girlfriend, grandson, daughter, parent, brother, baby, cousin, father, husband, sister, partner. c) 4 words have 3 syllables: family, fiancée, fiancé, granddaughter. d) 5 words have 4 syllables: father-in-law, brother-in-law, mother-in-law, foster parent, sister-in-law. e) 1 word has 6 syllables: adopted family.

4. 2 syllable words: all of the words have the strong stress on the first syllable: **boy**friend, **mo**ther, **grand**child, **grand**dad, **grand**ma, **ne**phew, **un**cle, **wo**man, **girl**friend, **grand**son, **daugh**ter, **par**ent, **bro**ther, **ba**by, **cou**sin, **fa**ther, **hus**band, **sis**ter, **part**ner. 3 syllable words: these words have the strong stress on the first syllable: **fam**ily, **grand**daughter; these words have the strong stress on the middle syllable: fi**an**cée, fi**an**cé. 4 syllable words: all of the words have the strong stress on the first syllable: **fa**ther-in-law, **bro**ther-in-law, **mo**ther-in-law, **fos**ter parent, **sis**ter-in-law. 6 syllable word: this word has the strong stress on the fourth syllable: adopted **fam**ily.

5. Adopted family, aunt, baby, boy, boyfriend, brother, brother-in-law, child, cousin, dad, daughter, ex-, family, father, father-in-law, fiancé, fiancée, foster parent, girl, girlfriend, grandchild, granddad, granddaughter, grandma, grandson, husband, man, mother, mother-in-law, mum, nephew, niece, parent, partner, sister, sister-in-law, son, uncle, wife, woman.

6. 2 letters: ex-. 3 letters: boy, dad, man, son, mum. 4 letters: aunt, baby, girl, wife. 5 letters: child, niece, uncle, woman. 6 letters: cousin, family, father, fiancé, mother, nephew, parent, sister. 7 letters: brother, fiancée, grandma, husband, partner. 8 letters: daughter, granddad, grandson. 9 letters: boyfriend. 10 letters: girlfriend, grandchild. 11 letters: father-in-law, mother-in-law, sister-in-law. 12 letters: brother-in-law, foster parent. 13 letters: adopted family, granddaughter.

7. See answer to number 5 above.

8. Answers will vary.

Sentence Blocks, Discussion Questions, Role Plays, Vocabulary Tests, Verb Forms Practice

Answers

Lesson Questions:

1. Answers will vary.

2. a) Aunt, daughter, fiancée, girl, girlfriend, granddaughter, grandma, mother, mother-in-law, mum, niece, sister, sister-in-law, wife, woman. b) boy, boyfriend, brother, brother-in-law, dad, father, father-in-law, fiancé, granddad, grandson, husband, man, nephew, son, uncle. c) baby, child, cousin, ex-, foster parent, grandchild, parent, partner.

3. Grandma.

4. Father-in-law.

5. Answers will vary. Suggested answers: a) baby, boy, brother, child, cousin, daughter, girl, grandchild, granddaughter, grandson, nephew, niece, sister, son. b) boyfriend, fiancé, fiancée, girlfriend. c) aunt, brother-in-law, dad, ex-, father, father-in-law, foster parent, husband, man, mother, mother-in-law, mum, parent, partner, sister-in-law, uncle, wife, woman. d) granddad, grandma.

6. Cousin.

7. Brother-in-law.

8. Adopted family, baby, boy, boyfriend, brother-in-law, child, ex-, father-in-law, fiancé, fiancée, foster parent, girl, girlfriend, husband, man, mother-in-law, partner, sister-in-law, wife, woman.

9. Granddaughter.

10. Ex-.

11. Partner.

12. a) Dad, b) aunt, c) baby, d) child, grandchild, e) son, f) niece.

13. Foster parent.

14. Adopted family.

Clothes:

General Questions:

1. Answers will vary.

2. Answers will vary.

3. a) 22 words have 1 syllable: ring, vest, tie, blouse, bra, dress, suit, pants, zip, tights, jeans, skirt, shorts, coat, scarf, sock, belt, shoe, top, shirt, hat, glove. b) 15 words have 2 syllables: slipper, tracksuit, buttons, earring, nightdress, trousers, high heels, t-shirt, jumper, necklace, glasses, knickers, jacket, trainer, handbag. c) 3 words have 3 syllables: underwear, pyjamas, uniform.

4. 2 syllable words: all of the words have the strong stress on the first syllable: **sli**pper, **track**suit, **butt**ons, **ear**ring, **night**dress, **trou**sers, **high** heels, **t**-shirt, **jum**per, **neck**lace, **glass**es, **knick**ers, **jack**et, **train**er, **hand**bag. 3 syllable words: these words have the strong stress on the first syllable: **uni**form, **un**derwear; this word has the strong stress on the middle syllable: py**ja**mas.

5. Belt, blouse, bra, buttons, coat, dress, earring, glasses, glove, handbag, hat, high heels, jacket, jeans, jumper, knickers, necklace, nightdress, pants, pyjamas, ring, scarf, shirt, shoe, shorts, skirt, slipper, sock, suit, tie, tights, top, tracksuit, trainer, trousers, t-shirt, underwear, uniform, vest, zip.

6. 3 letters: bra, hat, tie, top, zip. 4 letters: belt, coat, ring, shoe, sock, suit, vest. 5 letters: dress, glove, jeans, pants, scarf, shirt, skirt. 6 letters: blouse, jacket, jumper, shorts, tights, t-shirt. 7 letters: buttons, earring, glasses, handbag, pyjamas, slipper, trainer, uniform. 8 letters: knickers, necklace, trousers. 9 letters: high heels, tracksuit, underwear. 10 letters: nightdress.

Answers

7. See answer to number 5 above.

8. Answers will vary.

Lesson Questions:

1. Buttons.

2. Glasses.

3. Answers may vary. Suggested answer: blouse, bra, dress, handbag, high heels, knickers, tights, skirt, nightdress.

4. a) Ring, b) dress, c) shoe, d) slipper, e) scarf, f) glasses.

5. Shorts, top, tracksuit, trainer, t-shirt, vest.

6. Blouse.

7. Necklace, earring, ring.

8. Bra, vest, pants, sock, tights, underwear, knickers.

9. Bra, t-shirt, underwear, vest.

10. Slippers, socks.

11. Answers will vary. Suggested answers: clothes which are usually cheap: belt, blouse, bra, button, glove, hat, knickers, nightdress, pants, pyjamas, scarf, shirt, shorts, skirt, slipper, sock, suit, tie, tights, top, t-shirt, underwear, vest, zip. Clothes which are usually expensive: coat, dress, earring, glasses, handbag, high heels, jacket, necklace, ring, shoe, trainer, tracksuit, uniform, trousers, jeans, jumper.

12. Answers will vary. Suggested answer: knickers, nightdress, pants, vest, shorts, top, t-shirt, underwear, pyjamas.

13. Coat, glove, jacket, jumper, scarf, shoe, hat, trainer.

14. Ring.

Work:

General Questions:

1. Answers will vary.

2. Answers will vary.

3. a) 1 word has 1 syllable: nurse. b) 17 words have 2 syllables: plumber, farmer, jeweller, doctor, florist, artist, chauffeur, baker, actor, gardener, singer, teacher, soldier, builder, DJ, model, butcher. c) 11 words have 3 syllables: nursery nurse, pharmacist, manager, mechanic, accountant, hairdresser, optician, lecturer, head teacher, greengrocer, train driver. d) 6 words have 4 syllables: factory worker, sales assistant, electrician, estate agent, travel agent, receptionist. e) 3 words have 5 syllables: admin assistant, security guard, police officer. f) 1 word has 6 syllables: newspaper reporter. g) 1 word has 7 syllables: painter and decorator.

4. 2 syllable words: all of the words have the strong stress on the first syllable: **plumb**er, **farm**er, **jewell**er, **doc**tor, **flor**ist, **art**ist, **chauff**eur, **bak**er, **act**or, **gard**ener, **sing**er, **teach**er, **sold**ier, **build**er, **DJ**, **mod**el, **butch**er. 3 syllable words: these words have the strong stress on the first syllable: **nurs**ery nurse, **pharm**acist, **man**ager, **hair**dresser, **lec**turer, **green**grocer, **train** driver; these words have the strong stress on the middle syllable: head **teach**er, ac**count**ant, op**ti**cian, me**chan**ic. 4 syllable words: these words have the strong stress on the first syllable: **fac**tory worker, **sales** assistant, **trav**el agent; these words have the strong stress on the second syllable: es**tate** agent, re**cep**tionist; this word has the strong stress on the third syllable: elec**tri**cian. 5 syllable words: this word has the strong stress on the first syllable: **ad**min assistant; these words have the strong stress on the second syllable: se**cur**ity guard, po**lice** officer. 6 syllable word: this word has the strong stress on the first syllable: **news**paper reporter. 7 syllable word: this word has the strong stress on the fourth syllable: painter and **dec**orator.

Answers

5. Accountant, actor, admin assistant, artist, baker, builder, butcher, chauffeur, DJ, doctor, electrician, estate agent, factory worker, farmer, florist, gardener, greengrocer, hairdresser, head teacher, jeweller, lecturer, manager, mechanic, model, newspaper reporter, nurse, nursery nurse, optician, painter and decorator, pharmacist, plumber, police officer, receptionist, sales assistant, security guard, singer, soldier, teacher, train driver, travel agent.

6. 2 letters: DJ. 5 letters: actor, baker, model, nurse. 6 letters: artist, doctor, farmer, singer. 7 letters: builder, butcher, florist, manager, plumber, soldier, teacher. 8 letters: gardener, jeweller, lecturer, mechanic, optician. 9 letters: chauffeur. 10 letters: accountant, pharmacist. 11 letters: electrician, estate agent, greengrocer, hairdresser, head teacher, train driver, travel agent. 12 letters: nursery nurse, receptionist. 13 letters: factory worker, police officer, security guard. 14 letters: admin assistant, sales assistant. 17 letters: newspaper reporter. 19 letters: painter and decorator.

7. See answer to number 5 above.

8. Answers will vary.

Lesson Questions:

1. Plumber.

2. Florist.

3. Answers will vary. For example, most important jobs: doctor, nurse, police officer, teacher, farmer, etc.; least important jobs: DJ, model, etc.

4. DJ.

5. Estate agent.

6. Chauffeur, train driver.

7. Answers will vary. For example: a) manager, actor, DJ, doctor, optician, accountant, etc. b) admin assistant, nurse, pharmacist, travel agent, etc. c) artist, factory worker, nursery nurse, sales assistant, etc.

8. Jeweller.

9. Answers will vary.

10. Model.

11. Gardener.

12. Baker.

13. Answers will vary.

14. Answers will vary. For example, practical skills: builder, factory worker, farmer, plumber, gardener, police officer, etc.; intellectual skills: doctor, head teacher, lecturer, manager, newspaper reporter, optician, teacher, etc.

Home:

General Questions:

1. Answers will vary.

2. Answers will vary.

3. a) 12 words have 1 syllable: house, light, flat, door, stairs, wall, fridge, hall, floor, sink, bed, bath. b) 16 words have 2 syllables: carpet, bathroom, bedroom, cooker, cupboard, garden, fireplace, kitchen, garage, freezer, ceiling, sideboard, toilet, shower, sofa, wardrobe. c) 6 words have 3 syllables: apartment, detached house, bungalow, dining room, living room, dining chair. d) 4 words have 4 syllables: washing machine, radiator, television, dining table. e) 2 words have 5 syllables: DVD player, semi-detached house.

Answers

4. 2 syllable words: all of the words have the strong stress on the first syllable: **car**pet, **bath**room, **bed**room, **coo**ker, **cup**board, **gar**den, **fire**place, **kit**chen, **ga**rage, **free**zer, **cei**ling, **side**board, **toi**let, **sho**wer, **so**fa, **war**drobe. 3 syllable words: these words have the strong stress on the first syllable: **di**ning room, **bun**galow, **li**ving room, **di**ning chair; this word has the strong stress on the middle syllable: a**part**ment; this word has the strong stress on the last syllable: detached **house**. 4 syllable words: all of the words have the strong stress on the first syllable: **wa**shing machine, **ra**diator, **te**levision, **di**ning table. 5 syllable words: this word has the strong stress on the third syllable: DVD player; this word has the strong stress on the last syllable: semi-detached **house**.

5. Apartment, bath, bathroom, bed, bedroom, bungalow, carpet, ceiling, cooker, cupboard, detached house, dining chair, dining room, dining table, door, DVD player, fireplace, flat, floor, freezer, fridge, garage, garden, hall, house, kitchen, light, living room, radiator, semi-detached house, shower, sideboard, sink, sofa, stairs, television, toilet, wall, wardrobe, washing machine.

6. 3 letters: bed. 4 letters: bath, door, flat, hall, sink, sofa, wall. 5 letters: floor, house, light, stairs. 6 letters: carpet, cooker, fridge, garage, garden, shower, toilet. 7 letters: bedroom, ceiling, freezer, kitchen. 8 letters: bathroom, bungalow, cupboard, radiator, wardrobe. 9 letters: apartment, DVD player, fireplace, sideboard. 10 letters: dining room, living room, television. 11 letters: dining chair, dining table. 13 letters: detached house. 14 letters: washing machine. 17 letters: semi-detached house.

7. See answer to number 5 above.

8. Answers will vary.

Lesson Questions:

1. Stairs.

2. Hall.

3. a) Door, floor, b) sink, c) hall, wall, d) house, e) light, f) fridge.

4. Answers will vary. Suggested answer: flat, apartment, bungalow, house, semi-detached house, detached house.

5. Cupboard.

6. Dining room.

7. Kitchen.

8. Radiators.

9. Carpet.

10. Garden.

11. Ceiling.

12. Bath.

13. Answers will vary. Suggested answers: a) carpet, ceiling, cupboard, door, DVD player, fireplace, floor, wall, radiator, sofa, television, light. b) bath, ceiling, door, floor, light, wall, shower, sink, radiator. c) ceiling, cooker, cupboard, door, floor, freezer, fridge, light, radiator, sideboard, sink, wall, washing machine. d) carpet, ceiling, dining chair, dining table, door, fireplace, floor, light, wall, radiator. e) bed, carpet, ceiling, door, DVD player, floor, light, radiator, television, wall, wardrobe.

14. Walls.

Free Time:

General Questions:

1. Answers will vary.

Answers

2. Answers will vary.

3. a) 5 words have 1 syllable: tent, park, sport, golf, beach. b) 19 words have 2 syllables: tennis, fishing, cooking, camping, hobby, hiking, picnic, hotel, cycling, rugby, skiing, climbing, swimming, reading, weekend, football, café, playground, jogging. c) 10 words have 3 syllables: swimming pool, internet, cinema, volleyball, sleeping bag, holiday, theatre, bowling club, sunbathing, basketball. d) 6 words have 4 syllables: relaxation, computer game, leisure centre, watching TV, safari park, amusement park.

4. 2 syllable words: all of the words have the strong stress on the first syllable, apart from ho**tel**: **ten**nis, **fish**ing, **cook**ing, **cam**ping, **ho**bby, **hik**ing, **pic**nic, **cy**cling, **rug**by, **ski**ing, **cli**mbing, **swi**mming, **rea**ding, **week**end, **foot**ball, **café**, **play**ground, **jo**gging. 3 syllable words: all of the words have the strong stress on the first syllable: **swi**mming pool, **in**ternet, **ci**nema, **vo**lleyball, **slee**ping bag, **ho**liday, **thea**tre, **bow**ling club, **sun**bathing, **bas**ketball. 4 syllable words: these words have the strong stress on the first syllable: **wat**ching TV, **lei**sure centre; these words have the strong stress on the second syllable: com**pu**ter game, sa**fa**ri park, a**muse**ment park; this word has the strong stress on the third syllable: relax**a**tion.

5. Amusement park, basketball, beach, bowling club, café, camping, cinema, climbing, computer game, cooking, cycling, fishing, football, golf, hiking, hobby, holiday, hotel, internet, jogging, leisure centre, playground, park, picnic, reading, relaxation, rugby, safari park, skiing, sleeping bag, sport, sunbathing, swimming, swimming pool, tennis, tent, theatre, volleyball, watching TV, weekend.

6. 4 letters: café, golf, park, sport, tent. 5 letters: beach, hobby, hotel, rugby. 6 letters: cinema, hiking, picnic, skiing, tennis. 7 letters: camping, cooking, cycling, fishing, holiday, jogging, reading, theatre, weekend. 8 letters: climbing, football, internet, swimming. 10 letters: basketball, playground, relaxation, safari park, sunbathing, volleyball, watching TV. 11 letters: bowling club, sleeping bag. 12 letters: computer game, swimming pool. 13 letters: amusement park, leisure centre.

7. See answers to number 5 above.

8. Answers will vary.

Lesson Questions:

1. Safari park.

2. a) Park, b) sport, c) cooking, d) hotel, e) beach, f) tent.

3. Answers will vary. Suggested answer: basketball, climbing, volleyball, hiking, football, golf, jogging, leisure centre, playground, park, rugby, skiing, sport, swimming, swimming pool, tennis, cycling.

4. Amusement park, beach, bowling club, café, cinema, hotel, leisure centre, playground, park, theatre, swimming pool, tent, safari park.

5. Reading.

6. Camping.

7. Relaxation.

8. Answers will vary. Suggested answers: a) basketball, bowling club, café, cinema, computer game, cooking, hobby, hotel, internet, leisure centre, reading, relaxation, swimming, swimming pool, theatre, watching TV. b) volleyball, beach, camping, climbing, cooking, cycling, fishing, football, golf, hiking, hobby, jogging, playground, park, picnic, reading, relaxation, rugby, safari park, skiing, sleeping bag, sport, sunbathing, swimming, tennis, tent, amusement park.

9. Weekend.

10. Computer game.

11. a) Cinema, b) theatre.

12. Leisure centre.

Answers

13. Watching TV.

14. a) Basketball, climbing, cycling, fishing, football, golf, rugby, skiing, tennis, volleyball. b) Answers will vary.

Lesson Tests:

Town:

A) The syllable with the strong stress is marked in **bold**: a) **post** office (3 syllables). b) **li**brary (2 syllables). c) **ba**kery (3 syllables). d) **o**ffice (2 syllables). e) public **toi**lets (4 syllables).

B) 1. d), 2. a), 3. c).

C) 1. b) is different because the other words are shops or stores. 2. a) is different because the other words are connected with sport or exercise. 3. c) is different because the other words are things you could find in the street. 4. b) is different because the other words are places of worship.

D) Verb form: present perfect. 1. have. 2. Alex. 3. to meet. 4. have. 5. Jon. 6. haven't.

E) Verb form: future forms. 7. When. 8. Friday. 9. Will. 10. it. 11. Saturday. 12. won't.

Food and Drink:

A) a) milk. b) bread. c) cheese. d) fruit. e) chocolate. f) wine.

B) 1. eat. 2. can. 3. himself. 4. going. 5. just.

C) 1. cheese. 2. bread. 3. meat. 4. chips. 5. egg. 6. rice. 7. nut.

D) Verb form: present simple. 1. is. 2. bread. 3. Is. 4. it. 5. best. 6. isn't.

E) Verb form: first conditional. 7. What. 8. put on weight. 9. Will. 10. will. 11. lose weight. 12. No.

Shopping:

A) 1. e) groceries. 2. d) escalator. 3. a) manager. 4. f) checkout. 5. b) supermarket. 6. c) promotion.

B) 1. looked, everywhere, shop, tin, vegetable, soup, can't, find, anywhere. 2. Jan, leaving, car park, finished, shopping. 3. take, lift, fifth, floor. 4. Simon, visiting, new, shopping, centre, St. Mark's Road.

C) 1. price. 2. pence. 3. receipt. 4. bag. 5. pounds. 6. till. 7. sale.

D) Verb form: present simple. 1. Who. 2. is. 3. a small Italian restaurant. 4. she. 5. Is. 6. No.

E) Verb form: past simple. 7. use. 8. My. 9. Did you use. 10. did. 11. to. 12. didn't.

Health:

A) 1. **head**ache. 2. **ac**cident. 3. **ill**ness. 4. in**fec**tion. 5. e**mer**gency. 6. **am**bulance.

B) 1. is sitting. 2. is. 3. is going, visit. 4. phoned, make.

C) 1. The odd one out is **appointment**, because the other words are people. 2. The odd one out is **allergy**, because the other words are places. 3. The odd one out is **plaster**, because the other words are health problems. 4. The odd one out is **health**, because the other words all begin with the letter "p".

D) Verb form: modal verbs. 1. does. 2. Tomorrow. 3. Does. 4. does. 5. have to take. 6. doesn't.

E) Verb form: past continuous. 7. was. 8. Ella. 9. telling. 10. she. 11. Was. 12. No.

Answers

Transport:

A) 1. We've cancelled our flight because our daughter is ill. 2. Oliver was crossing the road when he was hit by a bus.

B) 1. is driving. 2. arrive, will. 3. cycle, get. 4. show.

C) The correct stress pattern is a).

D) Verb form: past simple. 1. do. 2. flew. 3. Did. 4. did. 5. go to. 6. No.

E) Verb form: present simple. 7. When or What time. 8. At. 9. you. 10. I. 11. Do. 12. don't.

Family:

A) 1. uncle. 2. sister, cousin. 3. nephew. 4. aunt, mum/mother.

B) 1. Incorrect. It should be: "**The whole family has** decided to go on holiday to Florida next year." 2. Correct.
3. Incorrect. It should be: "My sister was walking to the **city museum** with her children when she saw a **fox**."
4. Incorrect. It should be: "Jenna's aunt and uncle visited us in **May** because they wanted to see our new baby."

C) Answers will vary. Suggested answer: father, fiancée, girl, grandchild, husband, niece, partner, wife.

D) Verb form: modal verbs. 1. Whose. 2. Your. 3. my. 4. they. 5. Should. 6. shouldn't.

E) Verb form: present continuous. 7. is. 8. Playing. 9. Is. 10. is. 11. Roberto's daughter. 12. No.

Clothes:

A) 1. dress. 2. trousers. 3. uniform. 4. jacket. 5. glasses. 6. tie. 7. blouse.

B) 1. b) I wear glasses because I'm short-sighted. 2. d) We'll have a clearout of our wardrobe to see what we can give away to charity. 3. a) Stephen has to wear a blue and grey uniform every day for his job as a security guard.
4. c) If you wear a suit and tie to the interview you'll make an excellent impression.

C) 1. been. 2. but.

D) Verb form: past continuous. 1. was wearing. 2. was. 3. wearing. 4. he was. 5. Was. 6. wasn't wearing.

E) Verb form: present perfect. 7. have you always liked. 8. tops from Marks and Spencer. 9. Have. 10. have.
11. always. 12. I haven't always.

Work:

A) i) 1. Gerry, 2. hates, 3. working, 4. part-time, 5. dad's, 6. furniture, 7. business. ii) 1. friend, 2. Jo, 3. been,
4. unemployed, 5. last, 6. August.

B) 1. jeweller. 2. chauffeur. 3. estate agent. 4. builder. 5. nurse. 6. teacher. 7. factory worker. 8. actor.
9. hairdresser. 10. train driver. 11. accountant. 12. DJ.

C) 1. Edward (second time). 2. was. 3. is. 4. the.

D) Verb form: present continuous. 1. hoping to get promoted. 2. At the end. 3. Is. 4. Yes. 5. hoping to get. 6. she isn't.

E) Verb form: modal verbs. 7. What. 8. pay rise. 9. Do. 10. do. 11. I. 12. don't.

Home:

A) bath, bathroom, bungalow, carpet, ceiling, cooker, cupboard, door, fireplace, freezer, fridge.

B) 1. door, floor. 2. stairs. 3. light. 4. house. 5. shower. 6. hall, wall.

Answers

C) 1. showed. 2. machine. 3. you'll. 4. before. 5. watching. 6. night.

D) Verb form: present perfect. 1. What. 2. Cutting the grass. 3. Has. 4. has. 5. Jason finished. 6. hasn't.

E) Verb form: present simple. 7. do you. 8. In. 9. you. 10. I do. 11. Do. 12. don't live.

Free Time:

A) 1. camping. 2. theatre. 3. picnic. 4. climbing. 5. park. 6. swimming pool. 7. beach. 8. hotel. 9. reading. 10. café. 11. cooking. 12. sleeping bag.

B) 1. c) Chester's son was playing golf badly yesterday afternoon with a few friends from his cousin's bowling club. 2. a) I have seen Macbeth at this theatre five times. 3. d) Me, Jess and Casey are going to watch the tennis in the park. 4. b) I love going to the cinema with my friends, because we always have a good time.

C) Answers will vary. Suggested answer: camping, climbing, fishing, hiking, jogging, reading, sunbathing, swimming, tennis, volleyball.

D) Verb form: past simple. 1. did. 2. two weeks. 3. on. 4. we. 5. Did. 6. No.

E) Verb form: present continuous. 7. is. 8. Barney and Wanda are. 9. Are. 10. are. 11. Alex and Sue. 12. they aren't.

Sentence Stress

What is Sentence Stress?

Sentence stress is a natural part of spoken English and students should be encouraged to use it during the course. English is a stress-timed language which is spoken with rhythm. This results from strong and weak stresses that are built into both individual words and sentences. How can students recognise stresses in a sentence? The main rules for sentence stress in a *neutral* sentence (one without special emphasis) are as follows:

i) There are two kinds of word in most sentences: **content words** and **function words**. Content words are words that give the meaning in a sentence, such as **nouns** (e.g. bread), **main verbs** (e.g. eat, but not "be"), **adjectives** (e.g. sliced), **adverbs** (e.g. quickly), **numbers**, **wh- question words** (e.g. what), and **negative auxiliary verbs** (e.g. isn't). Function words are words that are essential to make the sentence grammatically correct, but don't have any intrinsic meaning on their own, i.e. without content words. They are words such as **pronouns** (e.g. she, them), **auxiliary verbs** (e.g. "are" in "They are going…"), **prepositions** (e.g. in, on), **articles** and **determiners** (e.g. a, the, some), **conjunctions** (e.g. and), **quantifiers** (e.g. many), and the **verb "be" when used as a main verb**. English native speakers may automatically *listen to* the content words in a sentence while *absorbing* the function words almost subconsciously.

ii) The strong stresses fall on the content words in a sentence while the weak stresses fall on the function words. If a word has a strong stress in a sentence it is spoken with more emphasis and volume, and more slowly than a word with a weak stress.

iii) The time between the stressed content words is the same, regardless of how many function words there are between them.

But does sentence stress matter? It's a difficult area – why not just leave it out? It can be a difficult concept for students to understand – particularly if their first language is not stress-timed, i.e. in their first language all the words in a sentence are spoken with equal stress. Native speakers of English speak quite naturally with sentence stress but if you asked one why they did this they would perhaps be unaware that they were even doing it, and at a loss to explain the rules (unless they had specifically studied the subject). Nevertheless, it is an important aspect of spoken English because when a student doesn't speak with sentence stress they can be hard to understand, even when what they're saying is grammatically correct and really interesting – a situation that can be quite frustrating for students. Understanding sentence stress can also help students to get more out of listening to spoken English.

On pages 137 to 139 we show the sentence stress in all eighty sentence block starting sentences from this course. The words in black are content words and have strong stress, while the words in grey are function words and have weak stress. There are many different ways that teachers can highlight sentence stress during the course of each lesson; below there are a handful of suggested activities to get the ball rolling. Let's use starting sentences from the "Food and Drink" topic in our examples.

Example with a Starting Sentence:

Michelle is having salad and pasta because she doesn't eat meat.

This sentence can be "translated" into weak and strong stresses like this:

Michelle is having salad and pasta because she doesn't eat meat.

The beats and the rhythm caused by the weak and strong stresses can be indicated like this:

Michelle is having salad and pasta because she doesn't eat meat.
●   ●   ●   ●   ●   ●   ●

So this starting sentence can be summarised in terms of sentence stress as simply:
●   ●   ●   ●   ●   ●   ●

In this starting sentence the content words are: Michelle (noun), having (main verb), salad (noun), pasta (noun), doesn't (negative auxiliary verb), eat (main verb), meat (noun). The function words are: is (auxiliary verb), and (conjunction), because (conjunction), she (personal pronoun). If you were to say the content words in order without

Sentence Stress

the function words, your listener could probably work out what you meant:

Michelle   having salad   pasta   doesn't eat meat.

Example with a Complete Sentence Block:

The best kind of bread is white sliced bread.
What

The sentences can be "translated" into weak and strong stresses like this:

The **best** kind of **bread** is **white** sliced **bread**.
What is the **best** kind of **bread**?
White sliced **bread**.
Is **white** sliced **bread** the **best** kind of **bread**?
Yes, it is.
Is **dry wholemeal bread** the **best** kind of **bread**?
No, it isn't. **Dry wholemeal bread** isn't the **best** kind of **bread**.

The beats and the rhythm caused by the weak and strong stresses can be indicated like this:

The **best** kind of **bread** is **white** sliced **bread**.
 ·   ●   ·   ●   ·   ●   ·   ●

What is the **best** kind of **bread**?
 ●   ·   ·   ●   ·   ·   ●

…and so on.

If you said only the content words, with rising intonation at the end of the yes/no questions, your listener would still get a good idea of your meaning:

    best   bread   white sliced bread.
What   best   bread?
White sliced bread.
   white sliced bread   best   bread? ↗
Yes
   dry wholemeal bread   best   bread? ↗
No,   isn't. Dry wholemeal bread isn't   best   bread.

Activities for Highlighting Sentence Stress:

- The teacher models the sentences and students repeat afterwards individually, in pairs, or as a group.
- The students mark on their handout the words in a sentence or sentence block that are content (stressed) and function (unstressed).
- The students record themselves saying starting sentences or sentence blocks with correct sentence stress, then listen back and check their work.
- The teacher (or a partner for pair work) says a starting sentence or sentence block and the listeners have to write only the content words or only the function words from it.
- The whole group (or pairs) have to recite sentence blocks (or individual sentences) as somebody claps, with the strong stresses falling on each clap and the weak stresses in between.
- The students have to form starting sentences or sentence blocks when they are given only the content words, or only the function words, and a given verb form.
- The students listen to songs, poems, or limericks and identify the content and function words; then practise repeating the lines with a partner or within the group.
- The students have to recite all the stressed words in a sentence block from memory.
- The students compile a list of content words and function words from a number of different sentence blocks, and put the words into groups, e.g. "noun", "main verb", "pronoun", "conjunction", "adjective", etc.

Sentence Stress

- Mumbling game: the students have to say a starting sentence or sentence block, not omitting the function words completely, but mumbling them so that they are barely heard. This can demonstrate quite well how native speakers of English stress the content words – the words which have meaning – but glide over the function words as if they were of little or no importance. (Yet the function words are critically important, particularly in an English language examination situation, because they are the glue sticking the content words together.)
- The teacher writes the content words from one sentence on separate cards (you could use the template on page 140 of this book) and the students have to put them in order, then fill in the missing function words.

A Note about Emphasis:

The arrangement of weak and strong stresses in a sentence can vary according to what the speaker wishes to emphasise. Look at this example:

Ellen was talking about her sister who loves fish and chips.   *Neutral – no special emphasis*

Ellen was talking about her sister who loves fish and chips.   *It is important <u>whose</u> sister Ellen was talking about*

Ellen was talking about her sister who loves fish and chips.   *It is important <u>when</u> Ellen was talking about her sister*

…and so on.

Sentence Blocks – Sentence Stress

Town:

1. Peter walks two kilometres to his office every day.
2. We're waiting patiently for the bus at the bus stop opposite the church.
3. Jennifer bought a couple of cakes at the bakery, then ran to the post office.
4. The department store was opening until 10 o'clock because they were having a massive sale.
5. I've agreed to meet Dan in the old market place outside the library.
6. We could drive to the lake and go fishing.
7. The new optician's next to the bank will open next Friday.
8. If the tennis court is busy we can go to the gym instead.

Food and Drink:

1. The best kind of bread is white sliced bread.
2. Michelle is having salad and pasta because she doesn't eat meat.
3. Daniel gave himself the largest portion of ice cream.
4. Ellen was talking about her sister who loves fish and chips.
5. Jenny has just put the cheese in the fridge.
6. Potatoes can be boiled, mashed, fried, chipped, roasted, or oven-baked.
7. We're going to buy some fruit at the supermarket this afternoon.
8. If you eat too much chocolate you will put on weight.

Shopping:

1. Emma is the manager of a small Italian restaurant.
2. Simon is visiting the new shopping centre near St. Mark's Road.
3. I used my debit card to buy a pair of shoes for work.
4. Jan was leaving the car park because she had finished her shopping.
5. I've looked everywhere in this shop for a tin of vegetable soup, but I can't find one anywhere.
6. We should take the lift to the fifth floor.
7. After we finish buying groceries we'll go to Nero's for a quick coffee.
8. If the checkout assistant offers to pack my bags I'll let her.

Health:

1. Being healthy is very important to me.
2. Sammi is sitting in the waiting room with her mum and brother.
3. I phoned my doctor this morning to make an appointment.
4. Ella was telling the receptionist about her husband's painful arthritis.
5. I've taken two tablets three times a day for a week, but I still don't feel any better.
6. Kenny has to take his prescription to the pharmacy tomorrow.
7. Simon is going to visit the optician's for an eye examination.
8. If you ask the doctor she will give you some good advice about your problem.

Sentence Blocks – Sentence Stress

Transport:

1. I usually get the train at 7.28.
2. Gemma is driving to the airport to pick up her grandmother.
3. I flew from Heathrow to Copenhagen last night.
4. Oliver was crossing the road when he was hit by a bus.
5. We've cancelled our flight because our daughter is ill.
6. All passengers must show their passports and boarding passes at the gate.
7. The next train to arrive at platform 8 will be the 9.49 service to Cardiff.
8. If we cycle to work we'll get there in about an hour.

Family:

1. My mum lives with her new partner in Brighton.
2. Roberto's daughter is playing with her cousins.
3. Jenna's aunt and uncle visited us in May because they wanted to see our new baby.
4. My sister was walking to the city museum with her children when she saw a fox.
5. The whole family has decided to go on holiday to Florida next year.
6. Your grandma and granddad should think about moving into a retirement bungalow.
7. Sam's brother is going to start university in Edinburgh next September.
8. If our parents get divorced the family will be very disappointed.

Clothes:

1. I wear glasses because I'm short-sighted.
2. Harry is trying on a new pair of smart black trousers.
3. Frankie bought herself a new dress and some underwear in the trendiest boutique on Oxford Street.
4. Michael was wearing the yellow and brown striped pyjamas that his grandma had knitted him for Christmas.
5. I have always liked jackets and tops from Marks and Spencer.
6. Stephen has to wear a blue and grey uniform every day for his job as a security guard.
7. We'll have a clearout of our wardrobe to see what we can give away to charity.
8. If you wear a suit and tie to the interview you'll make an excellent impression.

Work:

1. Gerry hates working part-time for his dad's furniture business.
2. Helena is hoping to get promoted at the end of the year.
3. When Greg worked for Dell he had to do plenty of overtime.
4. Edward was updating his CV because he wanted to apply for a new job.
5. My friend Jo has been unemployed since last August.
6. You need to ask your manager for a pay rise as soon as possible!
7. I'm going to visit that new employment agency about temporary work.
8. Dave will have to work very hard if he wants to have a successful career in sales.

Sentence Blocks – Sentence Stress

<u>Home:</u>

1. I live in a small semi-detached house in Manchester.
2. Mark is buying a new washing machine because his old one is broken.
3. When I went to their home Jack and Lisa showed me their new bathroom.
4. Sarah and Noel were watching funny DVDs in their living room for three hours last night.
5. Jason has finished cutting the grass in the back garden.
6. Barry has to do the washing up every night after tea.
7. I'll do the hoovering quickly before I have a bath.
8. If you sell your horrible flat you'll be able to put down a deposit on a nice house.

<u>Free Time:</u>

1. I love going to the cinema with my friends, because we always have a good time.
2. Barney and Wanda are enjoying a day out at an amusement park.
3. We went on a camping holiday last summer for two weeks.
4. Chester's son was playing golf badly yesterday afternoon with a few friends from his cousin's bowling club.
5. I have seen Macbeth at this theatre five times.
6. You should do some exercise instead of playing computer games all day.
7. Me, Jess and Casey are going to watch the tennis in the park.
8. If the leisure centre is still open we can all go swimming.

Sentence Blocks – Sentence Stress

Sentence Stress Activity Cards (see page 136)

Sentence Block Verbs from Elementary Book 1

All of these infinitive verbs are used to form the sentence blocks in this book. How many do you know? Write down a translation into your first language for each verb:

AGREE	_____	LOVE	_____
APPLY	_____	MAKE	_____
ARRIVE	_____	NEED	_____
ASK	_____	OFFER	_____
BE	_____	OPEN	_____
BUY	_____	PACK	_____
CANCEL	_____	PHONE	_____
CROSS	_____	PICK UP	_____
CUT	_____	PLAY	_____
CYCLE	_____	PUT	_____
DECIDE	_____	PUT DOWN	_____
DO	_____	PUT ON	_____
DRIVE	_____	RUN	_____
EAT	_____	SEE	_____
ENJOY	_____	SELL	_____
FEEL	_____	SHOW	_____
FIND	_____	SIT	_____
FINISH	_____	START	_____
FLY	_____	TAKE	_____
GET	_____	TALK	_____
GET DIVORCED	_____	TELL	_____
GET PROMOTED	_____	THINK	_____
GIVE	_____	TRY ON	_____
GIVE AWAY	_____	UPDATE	_____
GO	_____	USE	_____
HATE	_____	VISIT	_____
HAVE	_____	WAIT	_____
HIT	_____	WALK	_____
HOPE	_____	WANT	_____
KNIT	_____	WATCH	_____
LEAVE	_____	WEAR	_____
LET	_____	WORK	_____
LIKE	_____		
LIVE	_____		
LOOK	_____		

Discussion Words from Elementary Book 1

word	pronunciation	word	pronunciation
accident	/ˈæk.sɪ.dənt/	building	/ˈbɪl.dɪŋ/
accountant	/əˈkaʊn.tənt/	building site	/ˈbɪl.dɪŋ saɪt/
actor	/ˈæk.tə/	bungalow	/ˈbʌŋ.gəl.əʊ/
admin assistant	/ˈæd.mɪn əˈsɪs.tnt/	bus	/bʌs/
adopted family	/əˈdɒp.tɪd ˈfæm.ə.li/	bus stop	/bʌs stɒp/
aeroplane	/ˈeər.ə.pleɪn/	butcher	/ˈbʊtʃ.ə/
airport	/ˈeə.pɔːrt/	butter	/ˈbʌt.ə/
aisle	/aɪl/	buttons	/ˈbʌt.ənz/
allergy	/ˈæl.ə.dʒi/	café	/ˈkæf.eɪ/
ambulance	/ˈæm.bjʊ.lənts/	camping	/ˈkæm.pɪŋ/
amusement park	/əˈmjuːz.mənt pɑːk/	cancellation	/kænt.səlˈeɪ.ʃən/
apartment	/əˈpɑːt.mənt/	cancer	/ˈkænt.sə/
apartment block	/əˈpɑːt.mənt blɒk/	canoe	/kəˈnuː/
apple	/ˈæp.l/	car	/kɑː/
appointment	/əˈpɔɪnt.mənt/	car park	/ˈkɑː pɑːk/
artist	/ˈɑː.tɪst/	carpet	/ˈkɑː.pɪt/
aunt	/ɑːnt/	carrot	/ˈkær.ət/
baby	/ˈbeɪ.bi/	car showroom	/kɑː ˈʃəʊ.rʊm/
bag	/bæg/	cash	/kæʃ/
baker	/ˈbeɪ.kə/	cash point	/ˈkæʃ pɔɪnt/
bakery	/ˈbeɪ.kər.i/	casino	/kəˈsiː.nəʊ/
banana	/bəˈnɑː.nə/	cathedral	/kəˈθiː.drəl/
bank	/bæŋk/	ceiling	/ˈsiː.lɪŋ/
basketball	/ˈbɑː.skɪt.bɔːl/	cereal	/ˈsɪə.ri.əl/
bath	/bɑːθ/	change	/tʃeɪndʒ/
bathroom	/ˈbɑːθ.rʊm/	chauffeur	/ˈʃəʊ.fə/
beach	/biːtʃ/	checkout	/ˈtʃek.aʊt/
bed	/bed/	checkout assistant	/ˈtʃek.aʊt əˈsɪs.tənt/
bed and breakfast	/bed ənd ˈbrek.fəst/	cheese	/tʃiːz/
bedroom	/ˈbed.rʊm/	chemist	/ˈkem.ɪst/
beef	/biːf/	chicken	/ˈtʃɪk.ɪn/
belt	/belt/	child	/tʃaɪld/
bench	/bentʃ/	chips	/tʃɪps/
bike	/baɪk/	chocolate	/ˈtʃɒk.lət/
blouse	/blaʊz/	church	/tʃɜːtʃ/
boat	/bəʊt/	cinema	/ˈsɪn.ə.nə/
bookshop	/ˈbʊk.ʃɒp/	city	/ˈsɪt.i/
bowling club	/ˈbəʊ.lɪŋ klʌb/	climbing	/ˈklaɪ.mɪŋ/
boy	/bɔɪ/	clothes	/kləʊðz/
boyfriend	/ˈbɔɪ.frend/	clothes shop	/ˈkləʊðz ʃɒp/
bra	/brɑː/	coat	/kəʊt/
bread	/bred/	college	/ˈkɒl.ɪdʒ/
bridge	/brɪdʒ/	community centre	/kəˈmjuː.nə.ti ˈsen.tə/
broken bone	/ˈbrəʊ.kn ˈbəʊn/	commuter	/kəˈmjuː.tə/
brother	/ˈbrʌð.ə/	computer game	/kəmˈpjuː.tə geɪm/
brother-in-law	/ˈbrʌð.ə ɪn lɔː/	cooker	/ˈkʊk.ə/
bruise	/bruːz/	cooking	/ˈkʊk.ɪŋ/
builder	/ˈbɪl.də/	cousin	/ˈkʌz.ən/

Discussion Words from Elementary Book 1

crisps	/krɪsps/	fish	/fɪʃ/
cruise	/kruːz/	fishing	/ˈfɪʃ.ɪŋ/
crutch	/krʌtʃ/	flat	/flæt/
cupboard	/ˈkʌb.əd/	flight	/flaɪt/
customer	/ˈkʌs.tə.mə/	floor	/flɔː/
cut	/kʌt/	florist	/ˈflɒr.ɪst/
cycling	/ˈsaɪ.klɪŋ/	flour	/flaʊə/
dad	/dæd/	food	/fuːd/
daughter	/ˈdɔː.tə/	football	/ˈfʊt.bɔːl/
debit card	/ˈdeb.ɪt kɑːd/	football stadium	/ˈfʊt.bɔːl ˈsteɪ.di.əm/
delicatessen	/del.ɪ.kəˈtes.en/	foster parent	/ˈfɒs.tə ˈpeə.rənt/
dentist	/ˈden.tɪst/	free time	/friː taɪm/
department store	/dɪˈpɑːt.mənt stɔː/	freezer	/ˈfriː.zə/
detached house	/dɪˈtætʃt haʊs/	fridge	/frɪdʒ/
dining chair	/ˈdaɪ.nɪŋ tʃeə/	frozen food	/ˈfrəʊ.zen fuːd/
dining room	/ˈdaɪ.nɪŋ ruːm/	fruit	/fruːt/
dining table	/ˈdaɪ.nɪŋ ˈteɪ.bl/	fruit juice	/fruːt dʒuːs/
DJ	/ˈdiː.dʒeɪ/	garage	/ˈgær.ɑːʒ/
doctor	/ˈdɒk.tə/	garden	/ˈgɑː.dən/
door	/dɔː/	gardener	/ˈgɑːd.nə/
dress	/dres/	girl	/gɜːl/
drink	/drɪŋk/	girlfriend	/ˈgɜːl.frend/
driver	/ˈdraɪ.və/	glasses	/ˈglɑː.sɪz/
driving licence	/ˈdraɪ.vɪŋ ˈlaɪ.sənts/	glove	/glʌv/
DVD player	/diː.viːˈdiː ˈpleɪ.ə/	golf	/gɒlf/
earring	/ˈɪə.rɪŋ/	grandchild	/ˈgrænd.tʃaɪld/
egg	/eg/	granddad	/ˈgræn.dæd/
electrician	/ɪl.ekˈtrɪʃ.en/	granddaughter	/ˈgrænd.dɔː.tə/
emergency	/ɪˈmɜː.dʒənt.si/	grandma	/ˈgrænd.mɑː/
emergency exit	/ɪˈmɜː.dʒənt.si ˈek.sɪt/	grandson	/ˈgrænd.sʌn/
engine	/ˈen.dʒɪn/	greengrocer	/ˈgriːŋ.grəʊ.sə/
escalator	/ˈes.kə.leɪ.tə/	groceries	/ˈgrəʊ.sər.iːz/
estate agent	/ɪˈsteɪt ˈeɪ.dʒənt/	hairdresser	/ˈheə.dres.ə/
ex-	/eks/	hall	/hɔːl/
examination	/ɪg.zæm.ɪˈneɪ.ʃən/	handbag	/ˈhænd.bæg/
express lane	/ɪkˈspres leɪn/	hat	/hæt/
factory worker	/ˈfæk.tri ˈwɜː.kə/	headache	/ˈhed.eɪk/
family	/ˈfæm.əl.i/	head teacher	/ˈhed ˈtiː.tʃə/
fare	/feə/	health	/helθ/
farmer	/ˈfɑː.mə/	high heels	/haɪ hɪəlz/
father	/ˈfɑː.ðə/	hiking	/ˈhaɪ.kɪŋ/
father-in-law	/ˈfɑː.ðə ɪn lɔː/	hobby	/ˈhɒb.i/
ferry	/ˈfer.i/	holiday	/ˈhɒl.ɪ.deɪ/
fever	/ˈfiː.və/	holiday resort	/ˈhɒl.ɪ.deɪ rɪˈzɔːt/
fiancé	/fiˈɑːn.seɪ/	home	/həʊm/
fiancée	/fiˈɑːn.seɪ/	hospital	/ˈhɒs.pɪ.təl/
fine	/faɪn/	hotel	/həʊˈtel/
fireplace	/ˈfaɪə.pleɪs/	house	/haʊs/

Discussion Words from Elementary Book 1

word	IPA	word	IPA
husband	/ˈhʌz.bənd/	nursery nurse	/ˈnɜːs.ri nɜːs/
illness	/ˈɪl.nəs/	nut	/nʌt/
infection	/ɪnˈfek.ʃən/	office	/ˈɒf.ɪs/
injection	/ɪnˈdʒek.ʃən/	onion	/ˈʌn.jən/
internet	/ˈɪn.tə.net/	opening times	/ˈəʊ.pən.ɪŋ taɪmz/
jacket	/ˈdʒæk.ɪt/	optician	/ɒpˈtɪʃ.ən/
jeans	/dʒiːnz/	optician's	/ɒpˈtɪʃ.ənz/
jeweller	/ˈdʒuː.l.ə/	orange	/ˈɒr.ɪndʒ/
jogging	/ˈdʒɒg.ɪŋ/	painter and decorator	/ˈpeɪn.tə ən ˈdek.ər.eɪ.tə/
journey	/ˈdʒɜː.ni/	pants	/pænts/
jumper	/ˈdʒʌm.pə/	parent	/ˈpeə.rənt/
kitchen	/ˈkɪtʃ.ən/	park	/pɑːk/
knickers	/ˈnɪk.əz/	partner	/ˈpɑːt.nə/
lake	/leɪk/	passenger	/ˈpæs.ən.dʒə/
lamb	/læm/	pasta	/ˈpæs.tə/
lecturer	/ˈlek.tʃər.ə/	patient	/ˈpeɪ.ʃənt/
leisure centre	/ˈleʒ.ə ˈsen.tə/	pavement	/ˈpeɪv.mənt/
lemonade	/lem.əˈneɪd/	pence	/pents/
library	/ˈlaɪ.bri/	petrol pump	/ˈpet.rəl pʌmp/
lift	/lɪft/	pharmacist	/ˈfɑː.mə.sɪst/
light	/laɪt/	pharmacy	/ˈfɑː.mə.si/
living room	/ˈlɪv.ɪŋ ruːm/	picnic	/ˈpɪk.nɪk/
local shop	/ˈləʊ.kəl ʃɒp/	pie	/paɪ/
man	/mæn/	pizza	/ˈpiːt.sə/
manager	/ˈmæn.ɪ.dʒə/	plaster	/ˈplɑː.stə/
market	/ˈmɑː.kɪt/	playground	/ˈpleɪ.graʊnd/
market place	/ˈmɑː.kɪt pleɪs/	plumber	/ˈplʌm.ə/
meal	/mɪəl/	police officer	/pəˈliːs ˈɒf.ɪ.sə/
meat	/miːt/	police station	/pəˈliːs ˈsteɪ.ʃən/
mechanic	/məˈkæn.ɪk/	post office	/pəʊst ˈɒf.ɪs/
milk	/mɪlk/	potato	/pəˈteɪ.təʊ/
mineral water	/ˈmɪn.rəl ˈwɔː.tə/	pounds	/paʊndz/
model	/ˈmɒd.əl/	prescription	/prɪˈskrɪp.ʃən/
money	/ˈmʌn.i/	price	/praɪs/
mosque	/mɒsk/	problem	/ˈprɒb.ləm/
mother	/ˈmʌð.ə/	promotion	/prəˈməʊ.ʃən/
mother-in-law	/ˈmʌð.ə ɪn lɔː/	public toilets	/ˈpʌb.lɪk ˈtɔɪ.ləts/
motorbike	/ˈməʊ.tə.baɪk/	pyjamas	/pɪˈdʒɑː.məz/
motorway	/ˈməʊ.tə.weɪ/	queue	/kjuː/
mum	/mʌm/	radiator	/ˈreɪ.di.eɪ.tə/
mushroom	/ˈmʌʃ.ruːm/	rash	/ræʃ/
necklace	/ˈnek.ləs/	reading	/ˈriː.dɪŋ/
needle	/ˈniː.dl/	receipt	/rɪˈsiːt/
nephew	/ˈnef.juː/	receptionist	/rɪˈsep.ʃən.ɪst/
newspaper reporter	/ˈnjuːz.peɪ.pə rɪ.pɔː.tə/	refund	/ˈriː.fʌnd/
niece	/niːs/	relaxation	/riː.lækˈseɪ.ʃən/
nightdress	/ˈnaɪt.dres/	reservation	/rez.əˈveɪ.ʃən/
nurse	/nɜːs/	restaurant	/ˈres.tə.rɒnt/

Discussion Words from Elementary Book 1

rice	/raɪs/	stretcher	/ˈstretʃ.ə/
ring	/rɪŋ/	suit	/sjuːt/
river	/ˈrɪv.ə/	sunbathing	/ˈsʌn.beɪ.ðɪŋ/
road	/rəʊd/	supermarket	/ˈsuː.pə.mɑː.kɪt/
road sign	/rəʊd saɪn/	surgery	/ˈsɜː.dʒər.i/
roundabout	/ˈraʊnd.ə.baʊt/	swimming	/ˈswɪm.ɪŋ/
rugby	/ˈrʌg.bi/	swimming pool	/ˈswɪm.ɪŋ puːl/
runway	/ˈrʌn.weɪ/	tablets	/ˈtæb.ləts/
safari park	/səˈfɑː.ri pɑːk/	take-off	/ˈteɪk.ɒf/
sale	/seɪl/	taxi	/ˈtæk.si/
sales assistant	/seɪlz əˈsɪs.tənt/	tax office	/tæks ˈɒf.ɪs/
sausage	/ˈsɒs.ɪdʒ/	teacher	/ˈtiː.tʃə/
scales	/skeɪlz/	television	/ˈtel.ɪ.vɪʒ.ən/
scarf	/skɑːf/	tennis	/ˈten.ɪs/
school	/skuːl/	tennis court	/ˈten.ɪs kɔːt/
security guard	/sɪˈkjʊə.rɪ.ti gɑːd/	tent	/tent/
semi-detached house	/sem.i.dɪˈtætʃt haʊs/	theatre	/ˈθɪː.ə.tə/
service station	/ˈsɜː.vɪs ˈsteɪ.ʃən/	ticket	/ˈtɪk.ɪt/
shelf	/ʃelf/	tie	/taɪ/
ship	/ʃɪp/	tights	/taɪts/
shirt	/ʃɜːt/	till	/tɪl/
shoe	/ʃuː/	toilet	/ˈtɔɪ.lət/
shop	/ʃɒp/	tomato	/təˈmɑː.təʊ/
shopping	/ˈʃɒp.ɪŋ/	toothbrush	/ˈtuː.θ.brʌʃ/
shopping centre	/ˈʃɒp.ɪŋ ˈsen.tə/	toothpaste	/ˈtuː.θ.peɪst/
shorts	/ʃɔːts/	top	/tɒp/
shower	/ˈʃaʊ.ə/	town	/taʊn/
sideboard	/ˈsaɪd.bɔːd/	town hall	/taʊn hɔːl/
singer	/ˈsɪŋ.ə/	tracksuit	/ˈtræk.sjuːt/
sink	/sɪŋk/	tractor	/ˈtræk.tə/
sister	/ˈsɪs.tə/	traffic lights	/ˈtræf.ɪk laɪts/
sister-in-law	/ˈsɪs.tə ɪn lɔː/	train	/treɪn/
skiing	/ˈskiː.jɪŋ/	train driver	/treɪn ˈdraɪ.və/
skirt	/skɜːt/	trainer	/ˈtreɪ.nə/
sleeping bag	/ˈsliː.pɪŋ bæg/	transport	/ˈtræn.spɔːt/
slipper	/ˈslɪp.ə/	travel agent	/ˈtræv.əl ˈeɪ.dʒənt/
sock	/sɒk/	trolley	/ˈtrɒl.i/
sofa	/ˈsəʊ.fə/	trousers	/ˈtraʊ.zəz/
soldier	/ˈsəʊl.dʒə/	t-shirt	/ˈtiː.ʃɜːt/
son	/sʌn/	tyre	/taɪə/
soup	/suːp/	uncle	/ˈʌŋ.kl/
sport	/spɔːt/	underwear	/ˈʌn.də.weə/
stairs	/steəz/	uniform	/ˈjuː.nɪ.fɔːm/
station	/ˈsteɪ.ʃən/	university	/juː.nɪˈvɜː.sɪ.ti/
stethoscope	/ˈsteθ.ə.skəʊp/	van	/væn/
stitches	/ˈstɪtʃ.əz/	vegetable	/ˈvedʒ.tə.bl/
stomach ache	/ˈstʌm.ək.eɪk/	vest	/vest/
strawberry	/ˈstrɔː.ber.i/	village	/ˈvɪl.ɪdʒ/

Discussion Words from Elementary Book 1

volleyball	/ˈvɒl.i.bɔːl/
waiting room	/ˈweɪ.tɪŋ ruːm/
wall	/wɔːl/
wardrobe	/ˈwɔː.drəʊb/
washing machine	/ˈwɒʃ.ɪŋ məˈʃiːn/
watching TV	/ˈwɒtʃ.ɪŋ tiːˈviː/
water	/ˈwɔː.tə/
way in	/weɪˈɪn/
way out	/weɪˈaʊt/
weekend	/wiːkˈend/
wheelchair	/ˈwiːl.tʃeə/
wife	/waɪf/
wine	/waɪn/
woman	/ˈwʊm.ən/
work	/wɜːk/
x-ray	/ˈeks.reɪ/
zip	/zɪp/

My vocabulary words:

The 48 Sounds of English with the International Phonetic Alphabet (IPA)

23 Vowel Sounds: (8 short) (5 long) (10 diphthongs)

1.	ɪ	dish	/dɪʃ/	8.	iː	three	/θriː/
2.	æ	bat	/bæt/	9.	ɑː	star	/stɑː/
3.	ɒ	sock	/sɒk/	10.	ɔː	ball	/bɔːl/
4.	ʊ	pull	/pʊl/	11.	uː	shoot	/ʃuːt/
5.	ə	shoulder	/ˈʃəʊl.də/	12.	ɜː	shirt	/ʃɜːt/
6.	e	leg	/leg/	13.	ʌ	cup	/kʌp/
7.	i	happy	/ˈhæp.i/				

10 Diphthongs:

14.	eɪ	plane	/pleɪn/	19.	əʊ	home	/həʊm/
15.	aɪ	time	/taɪm/	20.	aʊ	cow	/kaʊ/
16.	ɔɪ	toy	/tɔɪ/	21.	ɪə	here	/hɪə/
17.	eə	pear	/peə/	22.	ʊə	pure	/pjʊə/
18.	aɪə	hire	/haɪə/	23.	aʊə	power	/paʊə/

25 Consonant Sounds: (15 voiced) (10 unvoiced)

24.	b	bag	/bæg/	37.	r	road	/rəʊd/
25.	g	glass	/glɑːs/	38.	w	week	/wiːk/
26.	v	van	/væn/	39.	j	yoghurt	/ˈjɒg.ət/
27.	t	taxi	/ˈtæk.si/	40.	m	music	/ˈmjuː.zɪk/
28.	d	dice	/daɪs/	41.	n	nurse	/nɜːs/
29.	θ	thousand	/ˈθaʊ.zənd/	42.	ŋ	ring	/rɪŋ/
30.	ð	brother	/ˈbrʌð.ə/	43.	l	lake	/leɪk/
31.	p	pig	/pɪg/	44.	f	frog	/frɒg/
32.	k	kit	/kɪt/	45.	z	zip	/zɪp/
33.	s	snow	/snəʊ/	46.	ʒ	revision	/rɪˈvɪʒ.ən/
34.	ʃ	shop	/ʃɒp/	47.	dʒ	jam	/dʒæm/
35.	tʃ	cheese	/tʃiːz/	48.	x	loch	/lɒx/
36.	h	head	/hed/				

Notes:
- *the syllable that follows this mark has strong stress:* ˈ
- *this mark denotes a division between syllables:* .

www.ingramcontent.com/pod-product-compliance
Lightning Source LLC
Chambersburg PA
CBHW081113080526
44587CB00021B/3582